Hooked Rugs  ay

Amy Oxford
Photography by Cynthia McAdoo

4880 Lower Valley Road, Atglen, PA 19310 USA

Dedication

Dedicated to the memory of Nancy Zickler
April 8, 1951 – December 21, 2003

Nancy's beautiful life and enthusiasm for the joy of
self-expression in the art form of rug hooking has
been a gift to each one of us. Thank you, Nancy.

Eye on the Sky. 12" by 14".
Designed and hooked by Nancy
Zickler as a part of the Green
Mountain Rug Hooking Guild's
2003 "Vermont Vignettes" project.

Library of Congress Cataloging-in-Publication Data

Oxford, Amy.
  Hooked rugs today / Amy Oxford ; photographs by Cynthia McAdoo.
    p. cm.
  ISBN 0-7643-2152-8 (pbk.)
  1. Rugs, Hooked—United States. I. Title.

NK2812.O96 2005
746.7'4'0973—dc22

                                    2004018154

Copyright © 2005 by Amy Oxford

Designed by "Sue"
Type set in Zapf Calligraphy BT/Souvenir Lt BT

ISBN: 0-7643-2152-8
Printed in China

Cover image: The Piano. Designed and hooked by Rae Reynolds Harrell.

*The photograph of Nancy Zickler is courtesy of Mary Florio with the help
of Ann Louise Smith. The picture of Nancy Zickler's "Vermont Vignette" is
courtesy of Anne-Marie Littenberg.*
*Background information on The Round Barn and Shelburne Museum
(page 8), © Shelburne Museum, Shelburne, Vermont.*
*Photographs taken in this book were taken in natural light with a Canon
10D digital camera and color adjusted in Adobe Photoshop.*
Rug measurements have been rounded off to the nearest inch.

Published by Schiffer Publishing Ltd.
4880 Lower Valley Road
Atglen, PA 19310
Phone: (610) 593-1777; Fax: (610) 593-2002
E-mail: Info@schifferbooks.com

For the largest selection of fine reference books on this and related subjects,
please visit our web site at **www.schifferbooks.com**
We are always looking for people to write books on new and related subjects.
If you have an idea for a book please contact us at the above address.

This book may be purchased from the publisher.
Include $3.95 for shipping.
Please try your bookstore first.
You may write for a free catalog.

In Europe, Schiffer books are distributed by
Bushwood Books
6 Marksbury Ave.
Kew Gardens
Surrey TW9 4JF England
Phone: 44 (0) 20 8392-8585; Fax: 44 (0) 20 8392-9876
E-mail: info@bushwoodbooks.co.uk
Free postage in the U.K., Europe; air mail at cost.

Contents

Acknowledgments 4
Foreword 5
A Brief History of the Green Mountain Rug Hooking Guild 6
Introduction 7
Chapter 1. Featured Artist – Jule Marie Smith 10
Chapter 2. The People's Choice Awards – 2004 22
Chapter 3. The People's Choice Awards – 2003 28
Chapter 4. In the Garden 34
Chapter 5. Animals 79
Chapter 6. Geometrics 119
Chapter 7. Pictorials 133
Chapter 8. Bags and Purses 185
Rug Show Vendors 189
Membership Information 190
Suggested Reading 191
Index 192

Can you find this chicken? She is hidden somewhere in this book in one of the rugs.

Acknowledgments

I would like to express sincere thanks to all the members of the Green Mountain Rug Hooking Guild. Your support for this project, your enthusiasm, encouragement, and the artistry you have brought to this rug show (and now to this book), have made my job a true pleasure. When the making of the book was announced, I knew that you would outdo yourselves creatively, but I never dreamed you would be so prolific. I am proud to be a member of such a supportive and talented guild.

Many thanks to my good friend and rug show co-chair, Celia Oliver. Without her, I couldn't have done the rug show once, not to mention twice. Her skills as an exhibit designer, her professionalism, and her ability to find easier ways of doing things always gave me confidence that we could pull it all off. It was wonderful having this excuse to spend so much time with her. Celia's help with the book was also invaluable.

Special thanks to Cynthia McAdoo for her expert job of photographing all of our rugs. When we got 175 more rugs than we were expecting, she never complained. We photographed in the outdoor entryway to the round barn for four and a half days. The lighting was excellent, but the temperatures were in the thirties. I'll never forget the image of Cynthia standing in front of her tripod and camera, with her parka, snow boots, and a sheepskin hat with the earflaps pulled down. Perched on top of an overturned flower pot – so she would be tall enough to get the perfect shot – she was covered in snow. I never could have done this book without her.

I am very grateful to my editors, Tina Skinner and Donna Baker, for their help and guidance.

Thank you to Shelburne Museum for being such gracious hosts for the last four years, and especially to Visitor Services Manager, Bruce Andrews. An honorary guild member, Bruce is a crucial part of our show.

Sincere thanks to the guild members who helped to photograph all the rugs: Jill Aiken, Jean Barber, Shirley Fortier, Rae Harrell, Jim Heininger, Priscilla Heininger, Cindy House, Bonnie LaPine, Sherry Lowe, Joyce Muller, and Maureen Yates. Your good cheer while freezing was remarkable.

The fact that this book has words, as well as pictures, is due completely to the dedication of guild members Nancy Bachand, Sara Burghoff, Gail Lapierre, Bonny LaPine, Karen Quigley, and Maureen Yates. They took the paperwork that arrived with all 625 rugs and typed up the details so each rug in the show could have its own label. Thanks to the Internet and the expertise of Maureen Yates, all these labels showed up one day on my computer, eager to become a book. Without these six women, the rugs seen here would have no names, and would all be made by Anonymous. Their stories would remain a secret.

I would like to express sincere gratitude to Anne-Marie Littenberg, and to my mother, Julie Righter, for proofreading; to Helen Wolfel, guild historian, for sharing her knowledge about the guild; to Patty Yoder for all of her detective work tracking down missing measurements and other wayward rug details; to Davey DeGraff, Cindy House, and Karen Kahle for making me laugh so hard; and to Lindsay Boyer, Mark Boyer, Burma Cassidy, Alaina Dickason, Lee Greenewalt, Bob Marley, Preston McAdoo, Peggy Mineau, Barb Moyer, Iris Oxford, Mat Oxford, John Soutter, Lucy Soutter, Nancy Urbanak, Sarah Urbanak, and Ed Wissner.

"The Vermont Turkey," hooked by Debbie Kirby, and "Checkerboard Cats," hooked by Dot Danforth, are both Warren Kimble images and appear with permission of Warren Kimble. "Mister Hare," hooked by Tricia Tague Miller, and "Yankee Clipper," hooked by Denise W. Jose, are also Warren Kimble images and are licensed patterns available through Barbara Carroll. Mr. Kimble's inspirational artwork and ongoing support of The Green Mountain Rug Hooking Guild are gratefully appreciated.

Heartfelt thanks to all of the guild members who volunteered at the rug show: Jill Aiken, Polly Alexander, Cosette Allen, Susan Andreson, Nancy Bachand, Carolyn Barney, Jean Barber, Nancy Birdsall, Jean Beard, Donna Beaudoin, Myles Beaudoin, Ann Berezowski, Betty Bouchard, Deb Boudriet, Loretta Bucceri, Kristina Burnett, Sara Burghoff, Shirley Chaiken, Annabelle Ciemiewicz, Jon Ciemiewicz, Willy Cochran, Linda Rae Coughlin, Jennifer Davey, Barbara Dawley, Davey DeGraff, Barbara Dewey, Suzanne Dirmaier, Judy Dodds, Lory Doolittle, Judy English, Fiona Fenwick, Maddy Fraioli, Shirley Fortier, Anne Frost, Ruth Frost, Robin Garcia, Sue Gault, Jane Griswold, Mary Ellen Hall, Jan Hammond, Sue Hammond, Dot Harder, Rae Harrell, Joan Hebert, Jim Heininger, Priscilla Heininger, Barbara Held, Ellie Hess, The Hinesburg Hookers, Sue Hommel, Cindy House, Marilyn Jackson, Lois Johnstone, Deborah Kaiser, Deb Kelley, Diane Kelly, Janet Knight, Stephanie Krauss, Jan Lacey, Gail Lapierre, Bonny LaPine, Jeanne Laplante, Jen Lavoie, Diane Learmonth, Diana Link, Anne-Marie Littenberg, Susan Longchamps, Sherry Lowe, Susan Mackey, Sandy Marquis, Karen Martin, Kris McDermet, Stewart McDermet, Joanne Miller, Joan Mohrmann, Diane Moore, Elizabeth Morgan, Joyce Muller, Bill Munson, Carol Munson, Joan Myers, Mary Lee O'Connor, Lynn Ocone, Fran Oken, Celia Oliver, Nora Oliver, Peter Oxford, George Palmer, Joanna Palmer, Jane Perry, Carol Petillo, Janice Peyton, Nancy Phillips, Bobbi Pond, Shelley Poremski, Suzi Prather, Karen Quigley, Judy Quintman, Dot Rankin, Gloria Reynolds, Emmy Robertson, Julie Rogers, Barbara Rosenthal, Arlene Scanlon, Gail Schmidt, Ginger Selman, Jim Selman, Lucinda Seward, Gwenn Smith, Jule Marie Smith, Amy Spokes, Ruth St. George, Monty Stokes, Cecelia Toth, Sharon Townsend, The Upper Valley Hookers, Nancy Urbanak, Johanna White, Ann Winterling, Patty Yoder, and Shirley Zandy.

Enormous thanks to my husband, Peter Oxford, for all his encouragement, support, patience, and good humor. Even when we lost our kitchen somewhere under the mountain of rug show registration forms he didn't complain. When all the rugs came down on the last day of the show he made an excellent bouncer, guarding the door and making sure that each rug went safely home where it belonged.

Foreword

We, the members of the Green Mountain Rug Hooking Guild, are so excited to be a part of this book. What could be better than pages and pages of wonderful hooked rugs, all done by members of our own guild? It is a dream that we never imagined, and we are ever amazed that it has come to pass.

Hooking has a strange power over a person. I am constantly hearing the same story when I ask, "How did you get started hooking?" The reply: "I saw a hooked rug (somewhere) and thought it might be interesting to see if I could do it. After some research I found a teacher and after about ten minutes of pulling the loops through the backing I was hooked. I have been hooking ever since and it has become a major part of my life." For some like myself, it has become a passion.

Not only does a person love the process of hooking, finding the wool and maybe dyeing it too, finding a pattern, or designing the project and pulling the loops, there is a whole other part as well. There is the camaraderie of just hooking together in groups weekly, monthly, or in classes. You meet people from all over the country who become your friends, real friends. You talk about hooking and you talk about your lives, your families, your history, and your future. Our guild's mission is to reach as many people as possible to encourage more participation in this art form we love. To accomplish this, we have a show every year.

For the past two years, Amy Oxford and Celia Oliver have chaired the event. 2004 was our best year ever. The overall quality of the workings of the show and the rugs themselves have moved to new heights. There were 625 rugs exhibited. As you read this book, you will see how the show takes on a life of its own, yet needs a huge amount of guidance by many people. Keeping all these people on course has been the expertise of Amy and Celia. Anne-Marie Littenberg has been another prime mover; she is the voice of the show, working all year on the publicity and then working weeks after as the treasurer. All of these women have a passion for hooking. They give of themselves to bring rug hooking to the attention of the public. Reading the book, or just looking at the pictures, you will see how important rug hooking is in the lives of those of us who share the love of wool and pulling or pushing loops. You will see the variety of interests of the people in our guild. They hook what they love. But what we all love is to hook.

—Patty Yoder
President, Green Mountain Rug Hooking Guild

A Brief History of the Green Mountain Rug Hooking Guild

Objectives of the Green Mountain Rug Hooking Guild: The objectives of this guild shall be to develop and promote interest in rug hooking; to maintain high standards and encourage creativity in this art form; to provide the means for an exchange of ideas and information among the members of the guild; and to promote educational activities to enhance the interest in and the quality of rug hooking.

The Green Mountain Rug Hooking Guild was founded in 1981 by a group of dedicated rug hookers. Guild historian Helen Wolfel of Barre, Vermont fondly remembers their first meeting, which was held at Vermont Technical College in Randolph, Vermont. "We met on the lawn and hung up our rugs on clotheslines. Everyone brought a picnic, and we selected our officers – that was our first meeting." Thirty-five people attended. "We wanted things to be very informal and kept things very simple," Helen says joking, "We were older and no one really wanted to do any work."

The guild became a member of ATHA (The Association of Traditional Hooking Artists). At least once a year, the guild was required by ATHA to have an exhibit that was open to the public. An ad was placed in the newspaper to spread the word and Helen recalls, "These exhibits became so well-known that people would come by the busload from all over. They would want to show their pieces, so they would become members, and the guild would grow. The guild wasn't very large for a number of years, but we always had at least seventy-five percent turn out. That's pretty good. We always had real enthusiasm, which has made it fun."

The guild would meet in town halls where they would bring a bag lunch, have their meeting, and enjoy an inspiring show and tell. They met at the Knights of Columbus Hall in Barre, Lum's Restaurant on the Barre Road in Barre, at The Hotel Coolidge in White River Junction, and at The Tavern in Montpelier, to name just a few places. For many years, they met at The Woodstock Inn, where, Helen says, "They treated us royally."

Helen, who was the first president of the Green Mountain Rug Hooking Guild and shared the presidency with Diana Boyd of Newfane, Vermont, said that over time the guild "needed new blood, young blood," and adds, "The new officers had access to copy machines and computers, which made things so much easier."

Meanwhile, the annual hooked rug exhibits were outgrowing all of the guild's meeting places. Current guild president, Patty Yoder, remembers that, "'Hooked in the Mountains' was the brainchild of Judy Phillips. At the fall meeting in 1995, guild president Suzanne Dirmaier called for new business. Judy stood up and, with great enthusiasm, proposed that we put together a rug hooking show for the following spring. Her idea was greeted with overall excitement and the show was born. A nucleus of six members seriously got the ball rolling. Kate Murray Jones quickly solved the first hurdle by finding the Round Barn in Waitsfield, Vermont. For five years, from 1996 to 2000, we held the rug show in the round barn with classes in outlying rooms. The first show had about 150 rugs."

While the first year's organizers at Waitsfield were nervous that they wouldn't have enough rugs to fill up the barn, four years later the yellow round barn was bursting at the seams. Classes were also overflowing and students had to be turned away. One classroom was a bright and sunny solarium complete with a long and skinny lap pool. When one unfortunate student fell in the pool, it became obvious that a move was in order.

In 2001, the rug show committee moved the show from one round barn to another, adopting The Round Barn at Shelburne Museum as its new home. The rugs had some breathing room and many historic buildings on the museum grounds were used as classrooms. Diane Phillips took on the job of organizing the classes, hiring the teachers, keeping the classes current, and keeping all who participate learning and happy.

Since 1981, the Green Mountain Rug Hooking Guild's membership has grown from 35 to 761. Members come from 36 states, Canada, and Japan. The rug show certainly has changed. From a picnic on the lawn to an elegant opening night reception with a jazz trio and gourmet food…the guild may have gotten fancier, but the important things remain the same. Helen Wolfel agrees, "It's wonderful how the guild has grown and what the guild has done for rug hooking. It's a very giving hobby. The members are very strong and close-knit. It provides an outlet to let you think about yourself, especially if you've been a housewife, a mother, or if you work. I can't say enough good things about the guild. We really love it."

Founding Members of The Green Mountain Rug Hooking Guild:

Anne Ashworth, W. Jean Armstrong, Janice Bean, Marie Beckers, Amparo A. Bliss, Anne Bond, Diana Boyd, Mary Burbank, Priscilla Buzzell, Grace Cook, Virginia Cook, Edista Cozzi, Helen Dumville, Jean B. Evans, Isabella Fiske, Arma Grearson, Helen M. Gregory, Helene Haines, Mary Hulette, Norma Ippolito, Beatrice R. Jewett, Louise S. Johnson, Pauline C. Manning, Anna Merriam, Mary Perolini, Mary E. Richards, Madalyn Richmond, Dorothy Savidge, Renee Scott, Lynda Starorypinski, Doris Stowell, Eva Sullivan, Ruth Vinton, Helen Wolfel, and Luise Wolfel.

Introduction

How This Book Came About

I was sitting at one of our semi-annual guild meetings. This one was held in the cafeteria at Shelburne Museum. The meeting was following the normal routine: the minutes from the last meeting were read by the secretary and then the president, vice president, and treasurer all gave their reports. "Any new business?" was asked, and of course, as usual, there was lots of new business. Next, Beverly Conway, the chairperson from the 2002 Hooked in the Mountains rug show, gave her wrap-up report about the recently completed show. At the end she told us that someone was needed to chair the show for the coming year. I remember thinking, "Gee, that would be really fun," reconsidering instantly with, "Are you crazy?" Beverly, trying to make the job sound easy said, "You know, it's not rocket science…" Encouraged, I thought, "I would love to do that," but again, the voice of reason jumped in saying, "I could never manage it all by myself." Then I looked across the room and saw my friend Celia Oliver sitting with a group of her buddies. Little did she know what was about to hit her.

I called her up the next day and we both decided that we were probably insane, and would hate ourselves later when things got busy, but that we would love to do it together anyway. The first thing we did was talk to Beverly to learn the ropes. We were given boxes of paperwork, dating back over many years, and were ready to get started.

Guild members debate whether or not it's a good thing, but the guild and the hooked rug show have grown tremendously since the first exhibit in 1981. It is now a major production to host this event, and we were told to expect around 400 rugs. We knew that the only way we could get the job done, without much gnashing of teeth and pulling of hair, was to break the show down into small tasks. All the things we could think of that needed to be done, big or small, from making coffee for the reception to hanging the lights for the show, were all written down. I don't know about you, but I have developed a fear of volunteering. Every nonprofit I've ever joined has been so starved for recruits that if you sign up to help at a fund raiser, the next thing you know you are head of the fund raiser, and then somehow you become treasurer, or president. We wanted our volunteers to know exactly what they were getting into, so they could pick a job that would be fun for them and that would fit into their schedules. At our guild meetings, and in our newsletter, we put out a call for volunteers, listing the many positions. At the end of the 2003 rug show, over 85 people had helped, some for a few hours and others for several weeks. "Many hands make light work" was our motto. This approach gave our event a real feeling of community and camaraderie. People who wanted to help now knew exactly how they could do it, and they were spectacular.

The 2003 show was a great success. Having done the show once, Celia and I were off the hook. We were relieved. I don't know whether something got slipped into our lemonade at the next meeting, or if we just got carried away with our own enthu-

siasm, but we agreed to do the show for a second year. It was at around this time that I got a call from my editor at Schiffer Publishing. She said, "I talked to our publisher and he said that although he didn't think your first book (*Punch Needle Rug Hooking*) would do very well because it is so different from anything we've ever done before, it turns out it's one of our best sellers. Would you like to do another book?"

At this point, I tried to act casual, nonchalant, calm, cool, and collected, when I really wanted to jump up and down screaming. I pulled myself together, and trying not to talk in a squeaky voice said, "I'd be happy to." I agreed to write a second book on punch needle rug hooking, but that night, I couldn't sleep. There was a third book that I really wanted to do. Every year when I attended our rug show, I always heard people asking for a brochure or program of the exhibit. It's very hard to find volunteers who have enough time to put together a program, especially under the time constraints that we work with to pull together the show. I also overheard people saying, "I wish I had a better camera," or, "If only I had more film," or, "Someone should really do a book about this show."

Having my editor call to ask me to do another book was a huge surprise. I figured that while they wanted me, which would surely only be a teeny window of time, I should ask to do an additional book. I screwed up my courage, called my editor, and gave her a rough outline of the rug show book. She said, "It sounds like a great idea." The project was approved and I decided to do this book first before jumping ahead to my next punch needle book.

I asked Cynthia McAdoo, of McAdoo Rugs, an expert hooked rug photographer who had worked on my first book, if she would like to collaborate again. She agreed wholeheartedly. Next, I approached our guild's membership at our 2003 fall meeting, to see if they thought the book was a good idea. After some debate, the book was approved enthusiastically. The guild voted to approve a grant to pay for film and developing costs and to give an honorarium to Cynthia.

> "We were expecting approximately 450 rugs, a few more than we had the year before. We got 625."

One of the benefits of being co-chair of the rug show is that you get to make up the rules. This worked very well when trying to coordinate throwing a book into the rug show mix. We were able to arrange to have two weeks between the day everyone dropped off their rugs at the round barn and the actual hanging of the show. This allowed time to photograph the rugs for the book. We were expecting approximately 450 rugs, a few more than we had the year before. We got 625. Some people said that having a chance to be in the book made them work more industriously than usual. The day arrived to install the show. For a while there was a bit of panic when it looked as if we were going to have more hooked rugs than walls to hang them on. Thanks to the skilled work of everyone who helped hang the show, a spot was found for each piece. Hanging a rug show is a bit like throwing a fancy dinner party. You want to make sure that everyone is seated next to someone they will get along with. When displaying our rugs, finding pieces that coordinate and complement each other is part of the challenge. With thirty-three people hanging the show, each one with an artistic eye, the results were breathtaking.

Welcome to the Rug Show – Hooked in the Mountains IX: April 17-25, 2004

The Round Barn, a three-story building measuring eighty feet in diameter, was constructed in 1901 by Fred "Silo" Quimby in East Passumpsic, Vermont. Round barns enjoyed a brief period of popularity in the late 19th and early 20th centuries. The first round barn in America was built by the Shakers in 1826, at Hancock, Massachusetts. The design was re-introduced in 1896 and building plans published in a nationally distributed farm journal sparked the construction of approximately twenty-four such barns in Vermont, beginning in 1899.

Economy of labor was the fundamental aim of round barn design. Hay, stored in the spacious top floor, and silage, stored in the central silo, could be easily dropped through feed chutes to the level below. There, up to sixty cows could be stanchioned around the center for feeding and milking. Manure was shoveled through trap doors to the basement where it could be collected by horse-drawn wagons.

The uppermost level of this barn is now used as Shelburne Museum's Visitor Orientation Center.

Shelburne Museum, founded in 1947, is one of the nation's most eclectic museums of art, Americana, architecture, and artifacts. Thirty-nine galleries and exhibition structures display over 150,000 objects spanning four centuries. Outstanding collections of folk art, decorative arts, tools, toys, textiles, and transportation vehicles are exhibited in tandem with paintings by artists such as Monet, Manet, Cassatt, Degas, Andrew Wyeth, Thomas Cole, Winslow Homer, Grandma Moses, and many others. The museum's twenty-five 19th-century structures include a covered bridge, a lighthouse, a 220 foot restored steamboat that is a National Historic Landmark, as well as the round barn that houses our rug show and other special events.

Originally displayed in the barn, and now included here, are 612 hooked pieces made by 293 people. Some entrants submitted one rug, others entered several, and the most prolific person brought twelve. For personal and copyright reasons, thirteen of the rugs from the show are not included here. Many rug hookers designed their own work, while others chose commercial patterns, many of which were purchased from our show's vendors in previous years. The smallest piece in the show, done with wool thread, measures just 1.75" by 1.75", while the largest, a bed rug, is 90" by 72". Rugs have been made by artists of all ages, from young children, to grandfathers, to great-grandmothers. In some cases, three generations of the same family are represented.

The Round Barn. © Shelburne Museum, Shelburne, Vermont.

The show is always so overwhelming, it seems impossible to see everything and soak it all in. You see dazed people walking around wide-eyed, with their jaws dropped, sometimes getting lost, and often talking to themselves. There never seems to be enough time to read all the labels that accompany the rugs, to admire each piece sufficiently, or to really see everything, no matter how many times you visit the exhibit. Of course, it would be much easier to concentrate if we didn't keep bumping into our friends, but then, that's half the fun.

Rug hooking offers many means of self-expression. In this book, you will find rugs that portray a multitude of subjects: the love of family, country, home, children, pets, flowers, history, wildlife, hobbies, and holidays, to name but a few. There are animals, both real and make-believe, rugs that tell a story, and rugs that make you laugh. They run the gamut: classic forms to abstracts, traditional to contemporary, fine art to decorative art, rugs for the floor and rugs for the wall. Some deal with difficult issues: war, terrorism, death, sorrow, and grief. Others rejoice in capturing the moments that make life sweet: bringing a newborn baby home from the hospital, dancing the tango, celebrating a wedding, playing the cello, and eating Dinty Moore Beef Stew cold from the can. You will find rugs that express the love of poetry as well as pieces that find joy and beauty in everyday things, from shoes to teapots. There are many surprises, including a dog wearing a party hat, a whale spouting a bouquet of flowers, and a sheep knitting her own sweater. Look for roses that seem so real, you can almost smell them, and scenes so unreal, you are happy to join the artist in imagining them. Memory rugs abound and capture things that are no more: a grandmother's kitchen, the family farm, a favorite pet, a childhood home, and a beloved 1938 Plymouth Coupe. What makes our guild so special is that our members are supported and encouraged, no matter what they make. Creativity is always nurtured. This is a splendid thing.

My goal for this book was to have it include every rug in the show, from the beginner's first small piece to the work of the most experienced rug hooking artist. No judges, no jury – just everyone. We are a group with talent, passion, enthusiasm, creativity, and a constant desire to improve our skills and our art. One of the things that sets our guild apart is our open-mindedness. We love the traditional and celebrate the rich historical heritage that came before us, but at the same time, we aren't afraid to try new things and make up new techniques. This book, an armchair version of the 2004 Hooked in The Mountains Exhibition, is a celebration of our love of rug hooking. I hope you enjoy it.

—Amy Oxford

Left and below left:
Hooked In The Mountains IX: An Exhibition Sponsored by The Green Mountain Rug Hooking Guild
April 17-25, 2004
The Round Barn. © Shelburne Museum
Shelburne, Vermont.

Hooked rugs hanging on the silo at the center of the round barn.

9

Chapter 1

Featured Artist – Jule Marie Smith

"From Here to There" – A Retrospective

Four years ago, the Green Mountain Rug Hooking Guild decided that they would like to recognize exceptional members of the guild whose artistic talent, and contributions to the rug hooking community have enriched our lives. Past featured artists include Patty Yoder, with her "Alphabet of Sheep" series; our guild's founding members (a special group exhibit); and rug hooking artist and teacher Dick LaBarge. This is one of the highest honors in our field, the "Oscar" of rug hooking. Featured artists take home the coveted "Wooley Bowl," a silver bowl engraved with a lovely sheep, their name, and the names of past honorees.

This year's featured artist, Jule Marie Smith, from Ballston Spa, New York, is a renowned fiber artist and widely respected as one of the finest rug hooking instructors in the world. Her work has been featured in numerous publications and her rugs have been showcased in many exhibits across the country. Her rug, "Trojan Moose," was the first place winner of our 2003 "People's Choice Award" and she has consistently been one of the top ten winners of this contest for many years.

Jule Marie works in wool with both linen and cotton backing. An expert dyer and a gifted designer, Smith is famous for her unusual and interesting borders. In this retrospective of her work, she describes her motivations and her inspirations. One thing is clear from reading the descriptions that follow: Jule Marie is fascinated by the process and the possibilities of hooked rug making. She talks repeatedly about the "games" she plays while hooking to entertain herself. There is an expression, "If a rug is boring to hook, it will probably be boring to look at." It is clear that Jule Marie Smith never gets bored when she hooks, and aren't we lucky?

Caricature of Jule. By Davey DeGraff and Rae Harrell, Hinesburg, Vermont. 1999. 14" by 12". "Making rugs is interwoven with the threads of my life. Like gardening, nurturing the colors of wool soothes and is necessary for a sense of happiness. Being part of the rug world has enriched my life manifold, and has brought me a wealth of friends, two of which presented me with this most wonderful gift, the caricature of 'Jule'."

Jule. Jule Marie Smith, Ballston Spa, New York. 2001. 13" by 21".

Featured artist Jule Marie Smith at the opening reception held in her honor, April 16, 2004. The Round Barn, Shelburne Museum.

Bessie Comes Home. Jule Marie Smith, Ballston Spa, New York. 2001. 38" by 52".
"Some rugs just happen. I wanted to do a red, many-windowed house, with an antique ark roof. The bird, star, 'deer dog,' trees, and irregular border shapes just came. Bessie was a dear woman in my mother-in-law's nursing home, who never had any visitors. While hooking, friends and I decided this was really an old rug hooker's home and Bessie's window is dark, as she is departing. But the attic window is the brightest, because all the hookers are going through Bessie's wool!"

About Jule Marie Smith

"This is my twenty-seventh year as a rug hooker. Have I become an old timer? I remember thinking, 'when I can finally do it, will anyone still be around?' I raised two sons, Geoffrey and Justin, and one daughter, Meredith, with rug hooking as my sanity. I got up at four a.m. to hook, because I needed my fix to start the day. I had an adult baby sitter and was able, with my husband's blessing, to go off to rug camp when my daughter was one."

"To my joy, people are still around! I have been fortunate to teach rug hooking for twenty years. These teaching experiences have led me to many different states and Canada. My rugs have been exhibited in numerous guild shows and major juried hooked rug shows in Massachusetts, Pennsylvania, New Jersey, and Mary-land. My work has appeared in *Rug Hooking Magazine* publications, in Leslie Linsley's *Hooked Rugs*, and in Jessie Turbayne's *Hooked Rug Treasury*. I live in the country, outside of Ballston Spa, New York, with my husband, Dan Smith."

My Style

"My style is to combine many hues and different textures and colors. A red outline in five different wools interests me more than a single-wool red outline. I am always trying to find my own balance. I love my many cutters but enjoy best, cutting by hand. My first teacher said we were following in the footsteps of our grandmothers who only had a basket of scraps, a hook, and scissors. I also draw my own rugs, like our grandmothers, who worked from their own minds and hearts."

Left and below:
Charlton Idyll. Jule Marie Smith, Ballston Spa, New York. 1983. 44" by 72".

Sweetman Road. Jule Marie Smith, Ballston Spa, New York. 1997. 13" by 70".

"I have lived on Sweetman Road in the town of Charlton for 34 years. While my worlds combine memory and fantasy, I do live in the yellow house. A neighbor's cows are often in the road and another neighbor drives her horses. The barn in both of these rugs is the old Sweetman Barn and has long since fallen down. In 'Charlton Idyll,' I hooked the church where I raised my children, next to an imagined graveyard, and placed my husband's childhood horses in the field."

Leaving Eden. Jule Marie Smith, Ballston Spa, New York. 2001. 37" by 67".
"I have long been interested in rugs made in the late 1800s, pouring over pictures of unusual, 'what was she thinking?' backgrounds. I wanted to do a primitive version of the Adam and Eve story. I drew motifs from antique furniture and imagination. I played the game of, 'This is all I have in my (large) basket, and when I run out, I'll pick up something similar.'"

The Crossing. Jule Marie Smith, Ballston Spa, New York. 2000. 52" by 64".
"From the beginning, I wanted all my rugs to have different borders. Making borders is another 'game' and a great place to learn about color and harmony. In 'The Crossing,' I wanted to experiment with big and bold, and a border larger than the interior. I had seen a deer cross my pond and I gave him two friends. I also had seen a tree in Maine with three crows in it. Like our grandmothers might have done when objects were getting lost, I surrounded the center motifs with off white."

Meredith's Sunflower Rug. Jule Marie Smith, Ballston Spa, New York. 2002. 31" by 49".
"Meredith has always loved sunflowers. Our only daughter, sometimes angelic, she is here with her dog and cat and our pond in the background. Again, the game was 'how many different sunflower centers can I make?' What is missing here is the giant flame border that I drew. No matter how I tried to make it work, it seemed too big and bold for a rug with large flowers, a medium angel, and small pond details. The learning was 'simple is better.'"

Bird in Hand. Jule Marie Smith, Ballston Spa, New York. 1995. 33" by 47".
"'Bird in Hand' was created after I had seen a folk art show with carvings of cows with birds on their backs. I could hardly wait to get home to do my reversal! This is also the first rug where I played with changing-color backgrounds. Note that the hands reach for crow faces, not the hearts."

Blue Horse. Jule Marie Smith, Ballston Spa, New York. 2002. 24" by 46".
"'Blue Horse' was, again, a journey into antique looking rugs, with random placement of mismatched shapes and animals. I drew this from templates created for an antique rug class and the purple brown deer is my favorite. I was trying for that faded out look of old rugs."

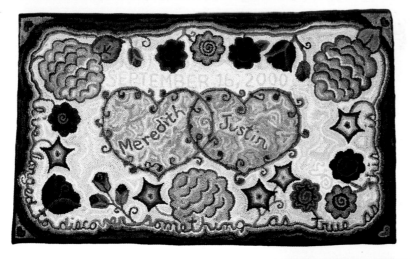

Left:
Justin and Merry's Wedding Rug.
Jule Marie Smith, Ballston Spa,
New York. 2001. 29" by 49".

Right:

Geoffrey and Sarah's Wedding Rug. Jule Marie Smith, Ballston Spa, New York. 2003. 29" by 49".

"It is so meaningful when rugs become personalized. 'Justin and Merry's Wedding Rug' is hooked in the wedding colors. The words in the border are from the song our own Meredith and son, Geoffrey, sang, during the ceremony."

"In 'Geoffrey and Sarah's Wedding Rug,' again there are the favorite colors of the bride, who is 'Sarah Bear' to her family. My son always loved monkeys so he became an ape. The whole rug is Colorado, where they live, a la Rousseau, complete with their dog/lion peering out from the ferns. And again, there are the words to the song that our Meredith and Justin sang at the wedding. (There *are* two Merediths in our family.)"

"While our children are now grown up, my son, Justin, used to sit with me and hook. My daughter, Meredith, still hooks with me. My favorite story about her is that she claims rights to all of the rugs I've hooked because she says she was around the most. I point out that each of my kids were there for eighteen years. She reiterates, 'yes, but I was there when you hooked the most.' So true! My kids do like my rugs and my family has been wonderfully supportive of Mom's thing."

Harold and Alice. Jule Marie Smith, Ballston Spa, New York. 1998. 36" by 62".
"I drew 'Harold and Alice' in memory of my father. The rug was completed for a rug show commemorating family memories, held in Wenham, Massachusetts. Harold and Alice are my parents who stand at center in their wedding pose. Their families of origin and birth homes are to either side. Brothers' and sisters' names are in the inner border. Family events and grandchildren are in the outer border. My parents were married in 1943, my dad went to war for two years, came back and raised a family, was the fire chief of our town, and died in 1992. This rug belongs to my mother."

A Gentleman's Fancy. Jule Marie Smith, Ballston Spa, New York. 1993. 41" by 82".
"'A Gentleman's Fancy' is a Patsy Becker design with my own border and my own 'courting' twist. There are ladybirds and gentlemen birds as well as horses. I began the rug in a primitive style with the bluebirds, but got fancy by the time I reached the cardinals!"

Geoffrey's Rug. Jule Marie Smith, Ballston Spa, New York. 1982. 37" by 68".
"'Geoffrey's Rug' is a very early rug, 1982, and probably the second rug I drew. Nine-year-old Geoffrey sits on the stone wall in front of our house, surrounded by his dog and cat. I was playing with scrolls and got that out of my system! In those early days I combined all my new learnings and dyeing into each rug."

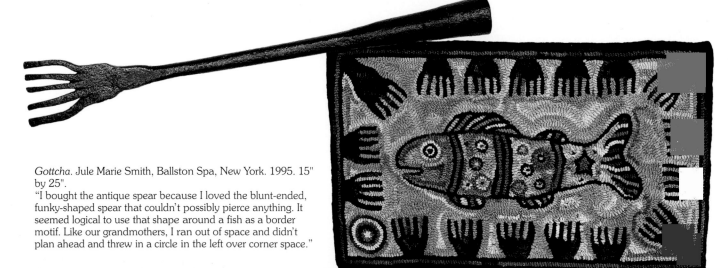

Gottcha. Jule Marie Smith, Ballston Spa, New York. 1995. 15" by 25".
"I bought the antique spear because I loved the blunt-ended, funky-shaped spear that couldn't possibly pierce anything. It seemed logical to use that shape around a fish as a border motif. Like our grandmothers, I ran out of space and didn't plan ahead and threw in a circle in the left over corner space."

Cat in Striped Pajamas. Jule Marie Smith, Ballston Spa, New York. 1996. 11" by 24".
"'Cat in Striped Pajamas' is a Vermont Folk Rug design that became my own with an evolving border that changed shape as it went around the rug."

15

Starry Starry Bird. Jule Marie Smith, Ballston Spa, New York. 2002. 26" by 17".
"'Starry Starry Bird' was a challenge rug for my classes. I gave each hooker the bird on the strange plant and each changed and recreated according to her fancy. We had Halloween birds on pumpkins and ghosts, and a robin on a nest, and bluebirds and roses. This striped fellow with another evolving border was my version."

Smith Family Hands. Jule Marie Smith, Ballston Spa, New York. 1999. 35" by 43".
"'Smith Family Hands' was an early play with all textures and is, of course, my family's hands. The game, which seems to be one of my favorites, was 'following shapes.' This rug has been on the floor in front of my kitchen sink, for five years!"

O Man. Jule Marie Smith, Ballston Spa, New York. 1997. 32" by 40".
"'O Man' was one of my first borders breaking out of the squared off places. I liked the stars and worked my irregular shape around them. Somehow the Greek Oracle boomed out of the heavens. The background was drag-dyed as that was my new dyeing technique of the time."

Flower Rooster. Jule Marie Smith, Ballston Spa, New York. 1977. 26" by 37".
"Everyone has a first rug. 'Flower Rooster' is mine and is a Lib Callaway design. I dyed the old skirts and made whatever colors appealed that day and I put them all in that first rug. This was my launching pad. It was 1976 and my teacher was Barbara Eshbach, who had a great hand in who I have become. Barbara was enthusiastic, warm, and so interested in sharing the primitive look found in early rugs and in the Kopp Book [*American Hooked & Sewn Rugs: Folk Art Underfoot*, by Joel and Kate Kopp]. She insisted upon one's own journey to find the answers and let me discover, myself, where to place colors. This kind of discovery is not pain free but it is true learning. Many, many thanks to you, Barbara."

16

Flower and Flame. Jule Marie Smith, Ballston Spa, New York. 1983. 46" by 70".

"I drew 'Flower and Flame' after watching the blue jays hanging upside down from my sunflowers. Color is truly 'everything'! One thinks of color in medium values. For the flames in the border, I had to dye very light and very dark and I learned a great deal about mediums AND light and dark for success in creating a flame border. Again, the only way to get around *that* many flames is to make sure the palette is large and no two flames are alike!"

Basket of Five. Jule Marie Smith, Ballston Spa, New York. 1996. 11" by 19".

Basket of Seven. Jule Marie Smith, Ballston Spa, New York. 1997. 16" by 25".

Star Flowers. Jule Marie Smith, Ballston Spa, New York. 2001. 26" by 39".

"I like baskets of flowers because one can really play with color combinations. I often make small things to entertain myself, fill a spot on the wall and illustrate an idea I have. These small baskets were in the vein of the old rugs. The larger basket of 'Star Flowers' was made for my bathroom, to match a wall sconce. Again, one of the games was a directional background."

Deer Dog Days. Jule Marie Smith, Ballston Spa, New York. 1996. 43" by 39".

Right:
Deer Runner. Jule Marie Smith, Ballston Spa, New York. 2002. 13" by 41".
"I was sitting in the doctor's office waiting for my daughter and fooling around, at Christmas time, with a deer drawing. That was my first squatty little deer dog. By the time the border came around, it had to be what deer dogs do on 'Deer Dog Days.' I haven't tired of deer and the 'Deer Runner' had to be made after I saw a runner made by a friend. It's great on a bench in my hallway."

Paws. Jule Marie Smith, Ballston Spa, New York. 1978-1981. 32" by 45".

Heart Flowers. Jule Marie Smith, Ballston Spa, New York. 1980. 36" by 36".

"These are very early rugs. I began 'Paws' in 1978 with Geoffrey and Justin's hands. Hooking time was limited and when Meredith was born in 1981, both boys' hands had grown and had to be drawn again. I actually put ink on my infant daughter's hands and took imprints for the baby book … and the rug! 'Heart Flowers' [right] is probably the first rug I drew and I was very interested in wide hand cut and funky old backgrounds. After twenty-four years on the floor and sun-fading, the rug actually looks antique!"

Samoset. Jule Marie Smith, Ballston Spa, New York. 1984. 24" by 28".

Yellow Bowl Rug. Jule Marie Smith, Ballston Spa, New York. 2003. 24" by 45".
"Many of my rugs are floor rugs, having that worn patina of being walked upon for years. 'Samoset' is a Lib Callaway design and an early piece. It was my first experiment with wild, big flowers. The background is all onion-dyed plaids. 'Yellow Bowl' is one of my last rugs completed and is all about my exploration of funky backgrounds. I am currently so intrigued by the helter-skelter wandering of color and shape."

Pandora's Box. Jule Marie Smith, Ballston Spa, New York. 1987. 16" by 39".
"I actually did the border first in 'Pandora's Box'. It came to me late that it would be a triptych and tell Pandora's story. The little bird appears three times: first, when all is lovely; second as he warns Pandora not to open the box! Last, he appears covering his eyes after the lid has been raised! I enjoy the 'game' of telling a story. 'How can I say *this*?'"

Two Angels. Jule Marie Smith, Ballston Spa, New York. 1996. 12" by 24".
"I did a series of two things facing each other: cats, cows, turkeys, foxes. It was fun making the cloud border in the 'Two Angels' rug, shading with a varied assortment of light and medium wools."

Assorted Coasters. Jule Marie Smith, Ballston Spa, New York. 2000. From 3" to 4.5".
"The coasters represent another game of entertaining myself. One can do an idea or a color plan quickly and simply in a coaster. These, by the way, are NOT for glasses! They sit in a yellow bowl!"

Too Cold to Fish. Jule Marie Smith, Ballston Spa, New York. 1994. 36" by 60".
"I made a series of large pictorial rugs which I sold. 'Too Cold to Fish' is mine. Again, it was personalized. The gentleman pushing the older lady is my father-in-law, with mother after her aneurysm and stroke. My daughter is the girl on the sled. Of course, a girl is winning the snowball fight! I used to say that borders should be quieter and enhance the inner rug. Dick LaBarge pointed out that I don't practice what I preach!"

Justin's Whale Rug. Jule Marie Smith, Ballston Spa, New York. 1985. 38" by 68".
"This was my first pictorial, completed after a trip watching whales off Cape Cod. In many ways it's hard to return to the naiveté of my early rugs as I became more schooled. Early attempts look most primitive in the antique style as it is where one figures out 'how'. Here I figured out how to do water, mashed potato clouds, and little people. A wonderful old child's blanket became the sails."

20

The Rape of Europa. Jule Marie Smith, Ballston Spa, New York. 1996. 39" by 36".
"I wanted 'The Rape of Europa' to be in the Cahoon Museum Show, 'Rugs of the Sea,' in Cotuit, Massachusetts. Being the most difficult rug I have drawn, it wasn't finished in time and I was allowed to show it as a work in progress. I chose the secondary colors and a drag-dyed background. Making such dissimilar border motifs was a challenge, as well as clouds that are orange, purple, and green. But again, great games are played, as Europa loses her shoe and flowers, and Triton and Neptune seem to cheer Zeus on. However, the sea nymphs are in total sympathy with their sister who is really *on the way* to the rape! The eyes of the Gods of Mount Olympus are in the Clouds. There is a suggestion of Hera's profile, as she looks away from Zeus' philandering."

Trojan Moose. Jule Marie Smith, Ballston Spa, New York. 2003. 48" by 51". First place winner of Hooked in the Mountain's People's Choice Award, 2003.
"After dwelling long in antique colors, friends and family were thinking I was becoming brown and gray. 'Trojan Moose' was my return to color. This rug was created for last year's 'Come Home to Vermont' theme for the Green Mountain Rug Hooking Guild Show. Since I don't live in Vermont, and live near Troy, New York, when I saw a Trojan horse picture, it came to me to wonder if there was a Troy, Vermont. There was, and Trojan Moose was born. This was one of my craziest borders and was a delight to work. Notice I haven't become bored with that large basket of many hues."

Chapter 2

The People's Choice Awards – 2004

Instead of having expert judges decide which rugs are the most deserving of recognition, we prefer to let the viewers choose. This year, when visitors arrived at our rug show they were given a small pink slip of paper – a ballot with these words: "People's Choice Award – Please Vote For Only One." The common response was, "What, only ONE?" This year, with 625 hooked pieces, it was especially hard to decide. The following ten rugs were voted best in show. Following tradition, these winning rugs will be invited back to be displayed in next year's Hooked in the Mountains exhibition. It is a great honor to be chosen by the public and by one's peers. Congratulations to this year's winners – your work is an inspiration.

2004 Winners

1. Jen Lavoie – *Lady on the Swing*
2. Patty Yoder – *Bailey's Got the Ball - Boots III*
3. Diane Moore – *Alphapets*
4. Karen Balon – *Double Trouble*
5. Suzanne Dirmaier – *Finish Your Work*
6. Rae Harrell – *The Piano*
7. Marty Dale Wagemaker – *With Flying Colors*
8. Emily Robertson – *English Garden*
9. Anne-Marie Littenberg – *Farm Garden With Distant Passing Storm*
10. Karen Balon – *Sleeping Goddess*

The People's Choice Award ballot box.

Lady on the Swing. People's Choice Award – First Place. Designed and hooked by Jen Lavoie, Huntington, Vermont. 29" by 44".

"'Lady on the Swing' was inspired by a real woman here in my town. I drove by her house almost every day. Every so often she would stop her incessant chores on the farm and sit quietly on her swing hanging from a huge old maple tree. I did not feel comfortable slowing down or taking her picture, so I asked my daughter to pose for the design. I had to embellish her figure because my daughter is quite thin and youthful. My goal was to hook her body the way she appeared to me – a strong, mature, hardworking farm woman.

I chose a night sky because it invoked so many different emotions for me. Such a long life, with so many milestones can only be truly appreciated in the stillness of the full moonlit sky. Eleanor Tomlinson passed away the week after I finished. I never got to show the rug to her, but I would like to dedicate it to her and all the beautiful old women who have inspired me. Just like the song by Michelle Shocked says, 'When I grow up I wanna be an old woman.'"

Bailey's Got the Ball - Boots III. People's Choice Award – Second Place. Designed and hooked by Patty Yoder, Tinmouth, Vermont. 66" x 66".

"We live in a household with three cats who have varied needs and personalities. I thought it would be fun to capture them at play. They are of different ages but their play level seems to match. I wanted this rug to also be a color study. I had a great time dyeing for and hooking our cats."

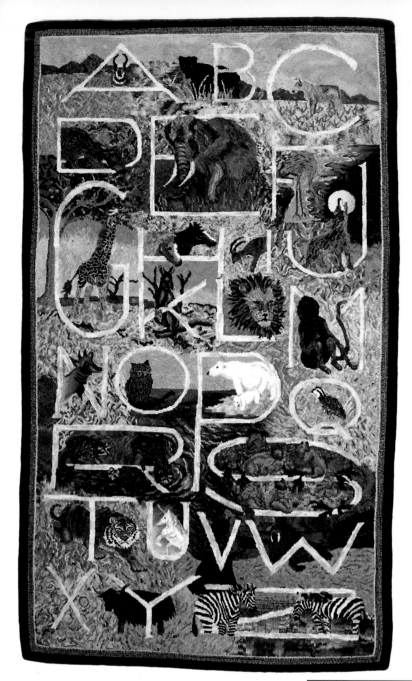

Finish Your Work. People's Choice Award – Fifth Place. Hooked by Suzanne Dirmaier, Waterbury Center, Vermont. 96" by 54". Designed by Suzanne Dirmaier and Susi Wilson.
"Sylvia Dole challenged me to do something bigger than my usual chair seat and voila, a 4' by 8' wildflower rug emerged. When I told Emmy Robertson that I had this rug that wasn't finished she looked me straight in the eye and admonished me to 'Finish your work!' It was fate. With her words ringing in my ears and the show date looming, I made a pact with myself to finish. I did, and thus its title."

Alphapets. People's Choice Award – Third Place. Hooked by Diane Moore, Morgan, Vermont. 55" by 32". Designed by Muzzy Petro.

Double Trouble. People's Choice Award – Fourth Place. Designed and hooked by Karen Balon, Goffstown, New Hampshire. 16" by 22".
"These two handsome boys were all the inspiration I needed to hook their portrait."

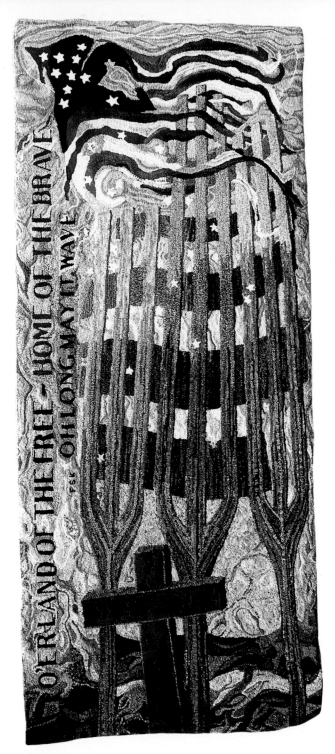

The Piano. People's Choice Award – Sixth Place. Designed and hooked by Rae Reynolds Harrell, Hinesburg, Vermont. 78" by 54". "Music has always inspired me. I feel joyful when listening and while I worked on this rug. As a result, I intend to create a whole orchestra that will encompass 25 or more rugs. We all know what I will be hooking for the next few years."

With Flying Colors - Homage to the World Trade Center. September 11, 2001. People's Choice Award – Seventh Place. Designed and hooked by Marty Dale Wagemaker, Palmyra, New York. 38" by 89".

With Flying Colors

Stained red wavelets swirl with the shed blood of courage.

Smokey white stars are the falling souls God is catching one by one.

Azure clear skies are streaked only with two piercing jet streams.

Why is freedom so frightening to those who do not share in it?

The silver towers have tarnished but will never disappear.

The imagery is forever.

Our faith, strength and love will only grow stronger and will build towers we cannot comprehend.

Our red, white, and blue will wave true to all.

©Marty Dale Wagemaker
March 25, 2004

25

English Garden. People's Choice Award – Eighth Place. Designed and hooked by Emily Robertson, Falmouth, Massachusetts. 50" by 36".

"The house and tree trunk are from a photo taken in England. I then added the rose bower and flower garden to frame the house. Fabric flowers have been added for visual interest as well as putting some of the flowers into the border."

Farm Garden With Distant Passing Storm. People's Choice Award – Ninth Place. Designed and hooked by Anne-Marie Littenberg, Burlington, Vermont. 21" by 39".
"The landscapes of Kansas and Missouri are astonishing: truck gardens, vast fields of grain and thunder storms that make the ones we get in the Green Mountains and Adirondacks seem petty. There are dozens of threads in each loop of this rug and over 100 loops per square inch. I work with a variety of punch needles."

Sleeping Goddess. People's Choice Award – Tenth Place. Designed and hooked by Karen Balon, Goffstown, New Hampshire. 51" by 26".
"I love hooking people and thought I'd make the piece more challenging by hooking a diaphanous gown."

Chapter 3

The People's Choice Awards – 2003

This year's hooked rug exhibit included the previous year's People's Choice Award winners. Back to take a final bow, these pieces deserve an encore. For a variety of reasons, not all of the winning rugs were able to be in this year's show. Out of the top ten winners, two people tied for fifth place and there was a three-way tie for sixth place.

2003 Winners

1. Jule Marie Smith – *Trojan Moose* (shown in Chapter 1)
2. Jon Ciemiewicz – *Majestic Ram*
3. Patty Yoder – *Steve Fish*
4. Lelia Ridgeway – *No One Ever Said Keeping a Promise Was Easy* (not shown)
5. Jen Lavoie – *Family Story*
5. Gail Lapierre – *Just Paddling Along*
6. Anne-Marie Littenberg – *Camel's Hump*
6. Abby Vakay – *My Boy's Backsides* (not shown)
6. Davey DeGraff – *Gerrit and Laura's Vermont Wedding*
7. Tricia Tague Miller – *Flying Hare*

Majestic Ram. Designed and hooked by Jon Ciemiewicz, Litchfield, New Hampshire. 24" by 24". People's Choice Award 2003.
"This rug was an adaptation of a public domain image found on the World Wide Web. The colors used were my concept of a bright light source illuminating the ram."

Steve Fish - Boots II. Designed and hooked by Patty Yoder, Tinmouth, Vermont. 34" by 60". People's Choice Award 2003.

Family Rug. Designed and hooked by Jen Lavoie, Huntington, Vermont. 82" by 34". People's Choice Award 2003.

Just Paddling Along. Designed and hooked by Gail Duclos Lapierre, Shelburne, Vermont. 43" by 30". People's Choice Award 2003.
"When I started this rug, I only had the canoe and paddlers in the center of a large piece of backing. I wasn't sure where I was going with it; it just evolved as I hooked it."

Camel's Hump. Designed and hooked by Anne-Marie Littenberg, Burlington, Vermont. 27" by 19". People's Choice Winner 2003.
"Camel's Hump is one of the Green Mountains. This was punch-hooked using dozens of plied threads."

Gerrit and Laura's Vermont Wedding. Hooked by Davey DeGraff, Hinesburg, Vermont. 54" by 36". Designed by Karen Kahle, Primitive Spirit, and Davey DeGraff. People's Choice Award 2003.

"This rug was adapted from Karen Kahle's 'Vermont' pattern. It was hooked for my son and his wife to stand on while they were being married last summer. It includes the wedding site (The Round Church in Richmond), the reception site (our camp and home on Lake Iroquois), and their new 'blue' house in Vergennes. They first saw this rug at last year's rug show."

Flying Hare. Hooked by Tricia Tague Miller, Alstead, New Hampshire. 32" by 44". Designed by Jan Gassner. People's Choice Award 2003.

"Since childhood I've loved rabbits and synchronicity produced this hooking. While at Dorr, I came upon this pattern and knew it was mine to do. In my wool stash lay a wonderful swatch of Jane Olson's, which was chosen as the core around which I would color plan. Most fun was hooking the rabbit, which was dip dyed. How this hare flies!"

Luise Wolfel: 2002 People's Choice Award Triple Winner

In the 2002 Hooked in the Mountains rug show, Luise Wolfel earned the distinction of having three of her rugs, "East Wind," "Provincial," and "Fantasia," all win the People's Choice Award. This is an incredible accomplishment. In poor health, Luise was unable to exhibit her winning rugs again in their place of honor at the 2003 show. When Luise's daughter-in-law, Helen Wolfel, asked if it would be possible to show her mother-in-law's rugs this year, we were thrilled to have them. Luise's beautiful color palette and her skilled use of fine shading set her work apart.

A founding member of the Green Mountain Rug Hooking Guild, Luise passed away a few weeks after the show, on May 15, 2004, at the age of ninety-three. She was born in 1910 in London, England, and entered the United States in 1929 via Ellis Island. Luise began making hooked rugs in 1966, studied with Leverne Brecia and Anne Ashworth, and was also a member of ATHA. Her daughter-in-law, Helen Wolfel, remembers, "Rug hooking was her life and she loved to share it. She was always willing to share a piece of wool or whatever anyone needed." Her enthusiasm for our guild, which she helped to launch, her love of rug hooking, and her generosity endeared her to all that had the good fortune to know her. Our triple crown winner, Luise Wolfel, will be sorely missed.

East Wind. Hooked by Luise Wolfel, Barre, Vermont. 32" by 41". Designed by Joan Moshimer. People's Choice Award 2002. Made in the 1960s or early 1970s.

Fantasia. Hooked by Luise Wolfel, Barre, Vermont. 79" by 42". Designed by Pearl McGown. People's Choice Award 2002.
"Leverne Brecia was Luise's teacher in New York. Luise hooked this picture in the late 1960s or early 1970s."

Provincial. Hooked by Luise Wolfel, Barre, Vermont. 94" by 42". Designed by Heirloom. People's Choice Award 2002. Made in the 1960s or early 1970s.

33

Chapter 4

In the Garden

Guild members are welcome to enter rugs depicting any subject into the show. Animals, geometrics, and pictorials of all kinds are always well represented. In addition to this, every year our rug show has a different theme. This year's theme, "In the Garden," challenged members to create a rug or other hooked piece with the garden in mind. The summer newsletter gave some suggestions: "While you are outside this summer, we hope this theme will inspire images of your favorite flowers or vegetables, a piece of garden sculpture or furniture, a landscaped yard or group of flower pots, the view of your garden from your porch, or the view from your garden. You be the designer!"

And design they did! We discovered that many rug hookers are also gardeners. It is no surprise, as arranging the colors and textures of a garden is very similar to color planning a rug. Each medium also has the attribute of evolving as it goes; flowers spread and send out volunteers, and rugs often start out as one thing and turn into a different variety altogether. Many guild members found that having a garden rug to hook in the depths of winter was just the ticket for the dreaded time of year when tomatoes are tasteless, the earth is frozen, and spring seems a long way off.

When we started setting up the rug show it was still snowing, but thanks to the help of donations from local businesses, volunteers used flowering plants, trees, shrubs, pussy willows, and silk flowers to transform the round barn into a summer's day. An arbor, picket fence, wheelbarrow overflowing with blooms, Adirondack chairs, bird baths, and vases full of hundreds of flowers set the stage for a pastoral walk "In the Garden."

If you have ever wondered where rug hookers get their inspiration, this book will give you lots of clues. When each rug was delivered to the show, it was accompanied by a form giving all the necessary details: name, address, phone number, rug title, size, etc. The form also requested the following information: "Source of Design (optional) – briefly describe (50-75 words) the inspiration for your design." Some people left this blank, others went far beyond the 75 words. All the artist's quotes included in this book come from this form.

My Garden Looking South. Designed and hooked by Joanna Palmer, Melrose, Massachusetts. 29" by 23".

Spring Phlox. Designed and hooked by Jennifer Davey, Thetford, Vermont. 21" by 16".
"These flowers were growing in my backyard last spring. I took many photos that day of various plants and buildings. I liked the idea of hooking a mostly green rug, trying to capture the elation we feel when green returns to Vermont."

In the Garden at Hilltop Farm. Designed and hooked by Ann Winterling, Concord, New Hampshire. 12" by 13".
"This tea cozy was inspired by my three visits to Beatrix Potter's charming cottage and garden called Hilltop Farm, Sawrey, the Lake District in England. I've always loved her stories, her biography, and her home and garden which appear in many of her stories."

Fairy Rug. Designed and hooked by Emily Robertson, Falmouth, Massachusetts. 54" by 36".
"I am always telling my friends and students to keep hooking because the fairies won't come to finish their work. This rug proves otherwise! I wanted to combine humor, light and shadow, lettering, and gardens into one rug. Here it is!"

How Does Your Garden Grow? Designed and hooked by Cynthia Richards, Pittsford, New York. 24" by 36".
"This rug was inspired by my love of gardening and need to wear a straw hat. I am always bending instead of kneeling. Hooked at Green Mountain Camp with Sherri Heiber-Day as my instructor."

Wistful Vista. Designed and hooked by Loretta Bucceri, Danby, Vermont. 34" by 19".
"Our new home requires new gardens. From my living room window this section of garden is visible. It's part reality and part of my 'wistful' imagination."

35

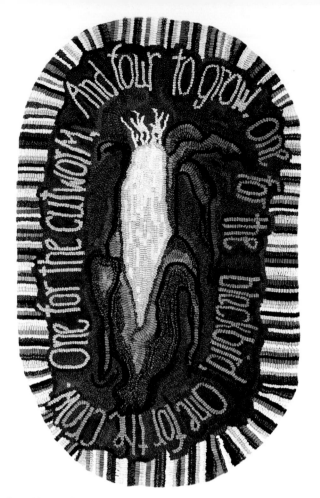

My Mother's Garden. Hooked by Norma Batastini, Glen Ridge, New Jersey. 27" by 20". Designed by Ellen Savage for Heart in Hand Rug Hooking.
"As a child growing up on a farm in Pennsylvania, a lot of time was spent in the family vegetable garden. Now the garden is much smaller and fenced in so animals don't raid the crop. It is tended by my mother, who also drew this pattern for me to hook. There are many memories in this rug, and yes, I do love veggies!"

Folk-Corn. Designed and hooked by Robin Wilson, Ridgefield, Connecticut. 27" by 43".
"My fond memories of my grandparents' corn field and also my fabulous collection of antique 'corn' Majolica pitchers and pieces inspired the design."

Corn Hill Monument. Designed and hooked by Miriam Henning, Truro, Massachusetts. 7" by 26".
"All summer I work at Corn Hill Beach in Truro, Massachusetts. All summer I answer tourists' questions and give them directions. Often their question is, 'Is there a monument or something that identifies Corn Hill?' I looked at the monument myself and took the corn and date for my mat."

Garland. Hooked by Priscilla Buzzell, Newport, Vermont. 36" by 25". Designed by Pearl McGown.
"A nice little floral. Always have enjoyed doing flowers. Background an interesting antique black."

Select Seeds. Designed and hooked by Sue Hammond, New London, New Hampshire. 19" by 41".
"This is an adaptation of an old advertising poster."

Watermelon Soft Sculpture. Designed and hooked by Susan Gault, Thetford Center, Vermont. 14" by 8".
"The Victorians decorated their homes with hand painted velvet fruit and vegetables. These decorative objects were the inspiration for my watermelon, which can also serve as a pillow."

Rippling Spray. Hooked by Barbara D. Pond, South Burlington, Vermont. 58" by 32". Designed by Pearl McGown.
"I saw this pattern several years ago at the Waitsfield Barn Show and searched till I found who designed it."

Shaded Rose Chair Seat. Hooked by Mary Jameson, Brattleboro, Vermont. 13" diameter. Design from Dorr Mill.
"First try at shading."

Gardening. Hooked by Ruth St. George, Shelburne, Vermont. 36" by 21". Designed by Beverly Conway Designs.

37

Gardening. Hooked by Eunice Whitney Heinlein, Avon, Connecticut. 36" by 22". Designed by Beverly Conway Designs.
"Inspiration for color plan – my gardener is a Red Hat lady."

Below:
Bowl of Strawberries Soft Sculpture. Designed and hooked by Susan Gault, Thetford Center, Vermont. Berry sizes range from 4" by 3.5" to 6" by 5.5".
"The Victorians decorated their homes with hand painted velvet fruit and vegetables. These decorative objects were the inspiration for my bowl of strawberries."

English Garden. Hooked by Phyllis M. Riley, Greenwich, New York. 48" by 32". Designed by Jeanne Field (Rittermere-Hurst).
"This was a rug I had wanted to do for several years. As luck would have it, I found the pattern in the Green Mountain Rug School's shop. It was difficult, but with the help of Nancy Blood, Jacqueline Hansen, and books, I struggled through."

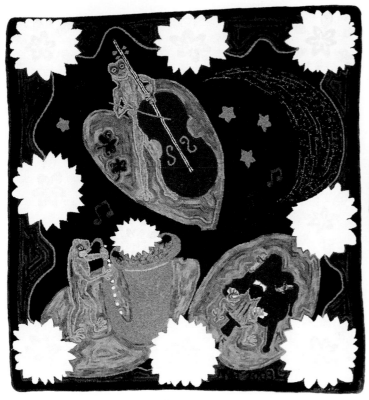

Swamp Boogie Nights. Hooked by Nancy D. Jewett, Pittsford, Vermont. 43"
by 40". Designed by Nancy D. Jewett for Fluff & Peachy Bean Designs.
"In my garden, night mist sprinkles her crystal droplets over sun-quenched
flowers, and shimmering petals, caressed with blossoming music, dance with
joy, in the night, in my garden."

Pansies. Hooked by Theresa Strack, Bedford, New Hampshire. 36" diameter.
Designed by Joan Moshimer.
"Each rug is a challenge of love for me. The pansies are dip-dyed with Pro
Chem dyes. I have had a great time completing this rug in time for the
exhibit."

Floral Bouquet. Hooked by Joan Wheeler,
Newport, Vermont. 18" by 19". Designed by
Jackye Hansen.
"I took Jackye's February class in Maine this year
to learn how to 'hove.'"

The Language of Herbs. Designed and hooked by Marilyn L. Sly, Mystic, Connecticut. 51" by 33".
"Since Elizabethan times, herb enthusiasts and romantic suitors have used flowers and herbs to convey
special messages. Meanings assigned to such plants are found in references for 'the language of flowers.'
As an herb lover, I chose to celebrate this tradition in my first rug design, bringing happy thoughts from
the garden into my home."

Right:
Winsome Faces. Hooked by Gloria Hautanen, North Truro, Massachusetts. 49" by 29". Designed by Pearl McGown.
"Lois Dugal dyed the wool for another rug for Gloria. Gloria changed her mind and made these pansies from that dyed wool."

Bottom:
National Bouquet. Hooked by Gloria Hautanen, North Truro, Massachusetts. 58" by 34". Designer unknown.
Baily Ruckert asks, "Gloria started this rug many years ago and just finished it this past year. Her favorite hooking theme was flowers. Gloria passed away before I could ask her who designed this pattern. Does anyone know?"

Blue Swan. Hooked by Gloria Hautanen, North Truro, Massachusetts. 26" by 20". Designed by Jon Ciemiewicz.
"Gloria always wanted to hook a swan and commissioned Jon Ciemiewicz to design one for her after seeing some of his work. She truly enjoyed his class."

—Baily Ruckert.

The Green Mountain Rug Hooking Guild is saddened to lose a very talented member of our guild. Gloria Hautanen, from Truro, Massachusetts, passed away this year at the age of sixty-two. A rug hooking teacher for over thirty years, a member of The Cranberry Chapter of ATHA, and a Certified McGown Instructor, Gloria's popularity can be attested to by the fact that many of her students had been coming to her for twenty-five years. Gloria taught in her home and at local adult education classes. She regularly took workshops from other rug hooking teachers to keep up with the latest trends in rug hooking and dyeing. She completed three rugs to enter in Hooked in the Mountains IX: "Winsome Faces," "Blue Swan," and "National Bouquet." One of Gloria's long time students, Baily Ruckert, brought her teacher's rugs to the show. Baily described Gloria as, "A good friend to all and an excellent teacher."

Pungent Pine. Hooked by Coren Moore Liang, Middletown, Connecticut. 25" by 34". Designed by Heirloom.
"A pine bough in the night sky with moonlight. I have my great-grandmother's hooked 'Pungent Pines' and now I also have this one made by me. They will look good together."

Below:
Lady Marion. Hooked by Mary Sargent, Johnson, Vermont. 30" by 21". Designed by Joan Moshimer.

In My Garden. Designed and hooked by Pat Merikallio, New Canaan, Connecticut. 34" by 26".
"My garden is pretty well destroyed by deer, so when the guild challenge came up, I thought I'd show my garden inside the deer."

Antique Rose Runner. Designed and hooked by Karen Kahle and Primitive Spirit, Eugene, Oregon. 53" by 20".
"I first created Antique Rose as a small 18" square pillow design, which was featured last year in *Rug Hooking Magazine*. I thought that it might be nice to put it on point and juxtapose it with geometric lines to give it an old-quilt feeling. This was my personal favorite of my 2004 designs."

Early Spring. Hooked by Sheila M. Breton, Surry, New Hampshire. 35" by 24". Designed by Jane McGown Flynn.

Rose and Tulip. Hooked by Sheila M. Breton, Surry, New Hampshire. 16" diameter. Designed by Pearl McGown.

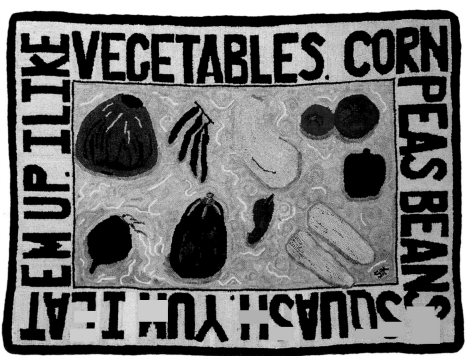

I Like Vegetables. Designed and hooked by Susan I. Koehler, Hopkinton, New Hampshire. 32" by 42".
"When my son, Chris, was in the fifth grade, he won a haiku contest with these words. I wanted to try hooking words plus this year's theme, 'In the Garden,' et voila!"

Poppies in the Garden. Designed and hooked by Mary Ellen Hall, Panton, Vermont. 23" by 36".
"Inspiration for this design came to me from my mom's flower garden. She has been gardening in the same spot for well over fifty years. There has always been a white picket fence around her garden to keep the rabbits out, she says. Although, she fondly recalls the babies that once took up residence beneath her pinks. Poppies bloomed beautifully …"

Bittersweet. Hooked by Robin Garcia, Calais, Vermont. 47" by 28". Designed by Stephanie Krauss for Green Mountain Hooked Rugs/Moxley Designs.
"I chose to adapt this original Moxley design of berries, vines, and leaves by adding flower petals (hulls) to the bittersweet berries. The border is created by using a straight stitch – different from the patterned stitch of the central background. These adaptations were made to add more life and color to the already vibrant design."

Left:
Summer. Hooked by Barbara D. Pond, South Burlington, Vermont. 35" by 25". Designed by Harry M. Fraser Company.
"Part of a series of the four seasons. I showed the other three at the guild's 2003 show."

French Oval. Hooked By Marion Dickie, Newbury, Vermont and Susan Mackey, Tinmouth, Vermont. 52" by 31". Designer unknown.
"In 1999, a friend of mine, Bridget Bowen, asked if I would be interested in seeing a hooked rug that was in a box in her attic. Her grandfather, Mr. Logan Dickie, who was eighty-four years old, had given it to her. His mother, Mrs. Marion Dickie, began the rug during the very early 1960s. She found, however, that her arthritis made the process of hooking very difficult. The box contained this rug, which I think is called 'French Oval.' Most of the flowers were completed and a very small corner of the scroll and gray background was begun. All of the wool for the flowers and scrollwork was still in the box, but there was not enough wool to do the background. The scroll was a red and black plaid dress. After conferring with Patty Yoder and Loretta Bucceri, fellow rug hookers, I followed their suggestion and did a black background. It has been an experience working on this piece because my preference is primitive folk art hooking. I feel honored to have been able to preserve a very special piece of artwork, and perhaps pass this on to Marion's great-great-grandchildren."
—Susan Mackey

Halifax. Hooked by Erika Egenes Anderson, Wesley Hills, New York. 24" by 36". Designed by Marion Ham – Quail Hill Designs.
"My very first rug, inspired by Marion Ham."

Aunt Mable. Hooked by Sandy Ducharme, Cabot, Vermont. 24" by 36". Designed by Stephanie Krauss for Green Mountain Hooked Rugs.
"This was my first rug hooking project and I purchased the design from Stephanie at Green Mountain Hooked Rugs."

Magnolias and Pussy Willows. Hooked by Colleen J. Miller, Grand Isle, Vermont. 50" by 32". Designed by Heirloom.
"I wanted to do a rug with swirling scrolls."

Caladium Mosaic. Hooked by Joan Mohrmann, Adirondack, New York. 80" by 36". Designed by Pearl McGown.
"An old odd McGown pattern that my daughter liked. I had my doubts. We color planned and as the pattern emerged, 'bloody eyeballs' came to mind. Lori loved it and placed it in her bedroom. I hadn't seen it in years when she brought it downstairs recently because of repair work being done upstairs. Suddenly, the old pattern appealed and I thought it would be fun to enter it in our show."

The Herbary. Hooked by Diane Burgess, Hinesburg, Vermont. 35" by 29". Designed by Karen Kahle and Primitive Spirit.
"Herb gardening is another passionate hobby of mine. I enjoyed hooking this new design for Karen Kahle's new Primitive Spirit catalog."

Floral Bouquet. Hooked by Coren Moore Liang, Middletown, Connecticut. 17" by 12". Designed by Jackye Hansen.
"I enjoyed Jackye's retreat, following her color design and pattern, and learning the Waldoboro style of hooking."

Hit and Miss Floral. Designed and hooked by Carole J. Ryan, Rutland, Vermont. 50" by 30".
"I wanted to use recycled and leftover wool from previous projects. I've always wanted to try hooking 'hit or miss' and found it easy to blend with a floral pattern."

My Melrose Floral. Hooked by Joanna Palmer, Melrose, Massachusetts. 61" by 27". Designed by George Palmer and Joanna Palmer.

Apple Tree Pear Trees Birds. Hooked by Dick LaBarge, Victory Mills, New York. 47" by 24". Designed by George Kahnle for Hooked on the Creek.
"Our philosophy is if one is good, more is better. So we have two birds in two pear trees plus apples and a few more birds to balance the design. Also proof you can shade in wide cut/ primitive using a variety of textured wools over dyed and carefully chosen."

Ivy in the Garden. Designed and hooked by Evelyn Haskell, East Wallingford, Vermont. 39" by 21".
"I wanted a simple design that would fit in anywhere."

Right:
A Vine of Flowers. Hooked by Deb Thomann, Gardner, Massachusetts. 29" by 18". Designer unknown.

My Mother's Garden. Designed and hooked by Sarah J. McNamara, Greenport, New York. 10" by 10".
"My mother grew many varieties of flowers, but my favorites were those in her shade garden. I hooked trillium, jack-in -the-pulpit, lily of the valley, and bleeding heart as a gift for her for Mother's Day 1996. The rubrum lily represents my sister Patty who spent several years in a coma before she died at the age of forty-seven. I'm sharing the mat this year in memory of my mother, Barbara Schurk McNamara, who passed away on January 1, 2004."

Fanciful Flowers. Designed and hooked by Dorothy Rankin, Monkton, Vermont. 18" by 25".
"The early rugs have a great appeal to me and inspired my design. But then the colorful flowers took over with dying and marbleizing wool, and the intriguing process of devising color combinations as I went along. An imaginary tree of flowers. What fun!"

Bird in Flowers and Leaves. Hooked by Evelyn Haskell, East Wallingford, Vermont. 29" by 21". Designed by Beverly Conway Designs.

Antique Posies. Hooked by Polly Reinhart, Wyomissing, Pennsylvania. 28" by 37". "This rug is a Barbara Carroll Pattern and was started in a Wooley Fox Workshop."

Great Granny's Garden. Hooked by Marilyn Jackson, Basking Ridge, New Jersey. 36" by 30". Designer unknown. "This is an antique pattern found in an antique store."

Jacobean Floral. Hooked by Cynthia Toolin, Enfield, Connecticut. 47" diameter. Design adapted from historic artwork.
"I love French country colors and Jacobean designs. The two come together for me in this rug."

Walter's. Designed and hooked by Molly W. Dye, Jacksonville, Vermont. 33" by 24".
"This is designed for my two-year-old grandson. It has trees that turn into stars and friendly animals that are at peace in the imaginary jungle. I wanted a happy atmosphere and one that he would be comfortable with. By the way, when Walter received the rug, he immediately put it on the floor and rolled himself up in it."

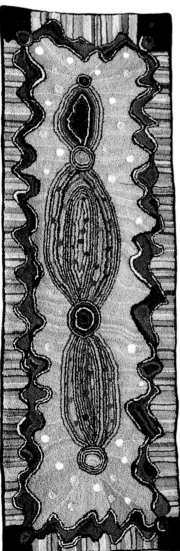

Outback Garden. Designed and hooked by Jean VanSchoonhoven Smith, New Bedford, Massachusetts. 87" by 28".
"Australian Aborigine designs are of great interest to me. I tried to capture the vigor and flickering quality I see in their use of color. The runner shape of my rug confines the garden plot of my outback garden."

Jungle Garden. Designed and hooked by Barbara Held, Tinmouth, Vermont. 32" by 26".
"I love bright colors and wanted to do some large flowers. I also love frogs and mushrooms and they all came together in this piece. The centers of the flowers are chenille and fleece and the edges are whipped in chenille."

Small Persian. Hooked by Peggy Stanilonis, Vergennes, Vermont. 35" by 22". Designed by Susan Feller – Ruckman Mill Farm.

Mini Fantasy. Hooked by Andrea Sargent, Johnson, Vermont. 33" by 24". Designed by Yankee Peddler.
"This is the second rug I started before I had a cutter so one half to three quarters of the rug is hand cut. My mom and I dyed a lot of the wool. Purple and green are my favorite colors together."

Dream Garden. Designed and hooked by Shirley Chaiken, Lebanon, New Hampshire. 25" by 46".
"This design is my adaptation of a needlepoint chart. That pattern used a section of the embroidery on a sofa from a manor house in England as inspiration."

Primitive Baskets. Hooked by Davey DeGraff, Hinesburg, Vermont. 39" by 23". Designed by Karen Kahle and Primitive Spirit.

Primitive Pineapple with Bees and Bee Skep. Hooked by Deb Thomann, Gardner, Massachusetts. 15" by 20". Designer unknown.

Left:
Dennis. Hooked by Gail Ferdinando, Pittstown, New Jersey. 28" by 42". Designed by Patsy Becker.

Lattice Garden. Designed and hooked by Judy Quintman, Wilmington, North Carolina. 63" by 27".
"I started this design at home and refined it in the class last year with George and Dick. I had fun using many scraps in the flowers and the border."

Protecting the Garden. Designed and hooked by Suzanne Dirmaier, Waterbury Center, Vermont. 50" by 25".
"Serious gardeners know that gardening in Vermont isn't all serenity. It has a dark side as well. One spring, after replanting my peas for the second time, I came unglued a la *Caddy Shack*. I tried all the remedies, mothballs, smoke bombs, you name it, to no avail. The only remedy remaining was what my father would describe as lead poisoning. 'Protecting the Garden' was born from the baser side of rural gardening."

Down Home. Designed and hooked by Carol Morris Petillo, Vinalhaven, Maine. 36" by 24".
"This rug tells the story of my happiest childhood memories 'down home' at my grandmother's house in central West Virginia. The house is gone now, as is my grandmother, who lovingly tended large gardens on either side of the house. There were always farm animals, and wild strawberries on the hillside in front. Her dog, Rover, was the first dog I ever loved, and he sits proudly in the middle, surveying his domain."

Grack's Palindromes. Hooked by Carol M. Munson, Sunderland, Vermont. 21" by 28". Design adapted from an antique hooked rug.

"My father took great pleasure in sharing palindromes with the grandchildren. They looked forward to the letters he sent addressed just to them. I started this rug in Emily Robertson's 'Humor in Rugs' class last year."

Below:

A Secret Garden. Hooked by Mary Hulette, South Burlington, Vermont. 31" by 32". Designed by Karen Kahle and Primitive Spirit.

"This rug was a wedding present for Aubrey Hallam. Aubrey was married to Gavin Boies in August 2003. Our family used to be neighbors with the Hallums and we have remained good friends with them through the years."

51

Aunt Polly's Roses. Designed and hooked by Susan Andreson, Newport Beach, California. 38" by 26".
"I copied a painting done by my friend, affectionately called 'Aunt Polly'. The picture of roses in her garden was painted about 1950. Aunt Polly challenged me to hook a rug to match. I completed the rug just after Aunt Polly's 100th birthday."

Fox Rug III – Summer Dawn (In My Imaginary Garden). Designed and hooked by Betty Oberstar, Wilton, Connecticut. 32" by 30".
"A red fox is one of my very favorite animals, and I have several times seen a lone fox or a pair in my yard in Connecticut. Some years ago I decided to design a series of fox rugs, one for each of the four seasons. This is the third rug. Rug number four is in progress."

After the Rain. Designed and hooked by Tracy Jamar, New York, New York. 28" by 23".
"Gardens look so wonderful after a rain – the colors bright against the stones and ground. I wondered what it would look like if the colors in flowers ran when they were wet. A variety of materials including, though not limited to, velvets, knits, metallics, silk, novelty yarns, as well as wool were used in this piece. I like the textural changes the materials create and thought it would be fun to go 3-D."

Old Monmouth. Hooked by Deborah Walsh, Cranford, New Jersey. 37" by 53".
Designed by Patsy Becker.
"I started this rug in a class with Patsy Becker at the Green Mountain Rug Hooking
School. She color-planned and dyed the wool for me. It was the first rug hooking
class I had taken and it was a lot of fun."

Autumn Leaves. Hooked by Susan Gingras,
Weybridge, Vermont. 77" by 43". Designed by
Nancy Urbanak of Beaver Brook Crafts.
"This rug is an adaptation of an antique rug. I
changed the pattern by making a diamond grid in
the middle. I just love this rug."

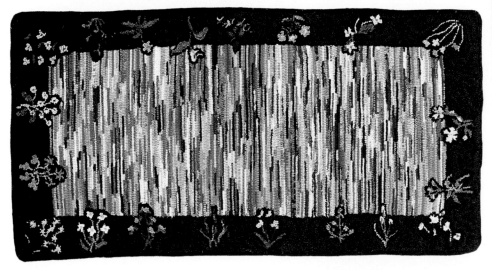

Worms in the Garden. Designed and hooked by Carol M. Munson, Sunderland, Vermont. 45" by 24".
"An overabundance of leftover 'worms' was the inspiration for this rug. I added the floral border in
hopes that spring would soon be here."

Joan's Garden. Designed and hooked by Joan DuBois-Frey,
Cornwall, Vermont. 69" by 50".
"I combined my love of 'scrap rugs' with the 'In the Garden'
theme for this year's rug show. I wanted to use my wealth of
pre-cut wool with an animal and flower motif. All the animals
pictured here, as well as the flowers, have made their way into
my garden at some point!"

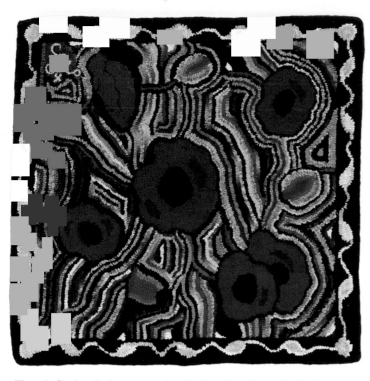

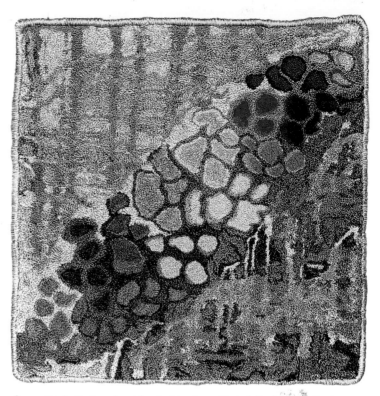

Wayne's Garden, II. Designed and hooked by Carol Morris Petillo, Vinalhaven, Maine. 30" by 30".
"The second rug I ever hooked was inspired by my husband's garden, which contained poppies, lilies, irises, nasturtiums, peonies, and many mistakes. I called it Wayne's Garden and despite its many problems, we enjoyed it very much. Now I plan to do a Wayne's Garden rug each year, emphasizing only one flower from the original rug, creating a series which, I hope, illustrates the advances I've made in technique."

Space Petals. Designed and hooked by Anne-Marie Littenberg, Burlington, Vermont. 19" by 19".
"This is my first color exploration where I used the color wheel. I wanted to achieve the effect where the background seems to be oozing and dripping. Thank you Jackson Pollack. This was punch-hooked using superfine threads where 20-30 are plied together for each loop. There are over 100 stitches (or loops) per square inch."

Chimera. Hooked by Becky Behrendt, Schenectady, New York. 39" by 52". Designed by New Earth Designs.

Right:
Garden Window. Designed and hooked by Barbara Held, Tinmouth, Vermont. 37" by 22".
"The rainbow dyed wool inspired this rug, along with a desire to do an abstract. The long fringe is a macramé holdover and is meant to give the feel of curtains. My garden view is ever-changing, as is the view through this window."

Grandmother's Flower Garden. Hooked by Patti Varley, Saratoga Springs, New York. 49" by 27". Designed by Lib Callaway.

Memories in My Garden. Designed and hooked by Jane Griswold, Rutland, Vermont. 36" by 22".
"I designed this rug to honor people in my family who have passed away. Their initials are hooked into the ground part of the rug and I was reminded of some wonderful memories as I hooked this rug."

Untitled #1. Designed and hooked by Lucinda Seward, Pittsford, Vermont. 30" by 58".
"This rug was adapted from an antique rug that we bought and resold through our antique business."

55

Exotica. Hooked by Tricia Tague Miller, Alstead, New Hampshire. 45" by 34". Designed by Jane Olson.
"A change was in order! With guidance and suggestions from both Jane and Nancy Blood, 'Exotica' evolved, altered somewhat from the original pattern – yet quite exotic."

Meditation Garden. Designed and hooked by Mary Lee O'Connor, Ballston Spa, New York. 24" by 22".
"At the 2003 Shelburne class taught by Rae Harrell, Rae had us meditate. This rug depicts where I went during the meditation. I sat on a log, in a field, surrounded by flowers and trees with the sun on my face."

African Daisies. Designed and hooked by Noriko Manago, Kumano-shi, Japan. 33" by 39".
"I started sketching African daisies for days for my rug design. One day I found a little hole on the leaf of a real flower. A bell rang in my head. 'Ding Dong!' What if a flower came up from this hole? My imagination suddenly came alive. In my rug, inchworms on the leaves are busy eating and earthworms are happily crawling on the ground."

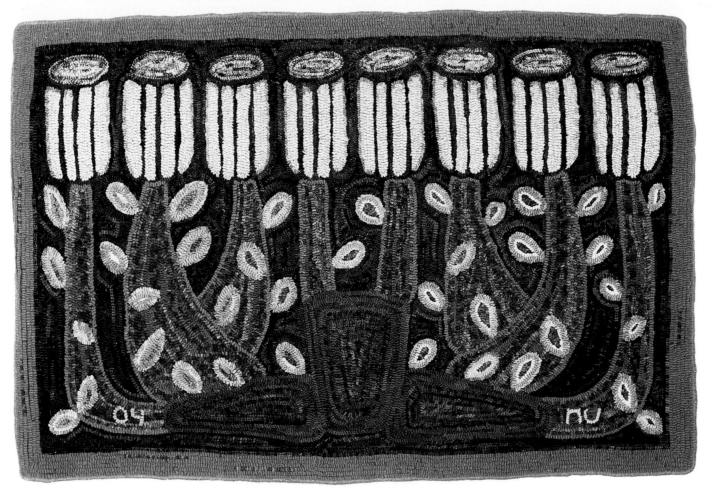

Dandy Lion. Hooked by Nancy Urbanak, Cornwall, Vermont. 48" by 33". Designed by Red Clover Rugs.
"I thought this primitive design was very interesting and different from anything I'd hooked before. After making a few modifications, I decided on a blue background and chose #63, Jack Boy Blue, from *Antique Colors for Primitive Rugs,* by Barbara Carroll and Emma Lou Lais. The other colors fell into place and the rug hooked up very quickly."

A Rose Is a Rose. Hooked by Jean W. Beard, Hanover, New Hampshire. 36" by 25". Designer unknown.
"I was given this pattern quite a few years ago by someone who was giving up their hobby of hooking."

Fall. Hooked and adapted by Joanna Henderson, Hopkinton, New Hampshire. 30" by 41".
"I saw a photograph of an antique rug in a magazine which inspired me to make the rug, with some changes."

57

Quim. Hooked by Evelyn Haskell, East Wallingford, Vermont. 27" by 20". Designer unknown.

Angel in the Garden. Hooked by Cheryl Connor, Bridport, Vermont. 17" by 15". Designed by Cheryl Connor and Sharon Thompson.
"This chair pad is the fourth pad I have made for my square dining room chairs. The flowers and the body of the angel are hooked traditionally. The background and stems are punch hooked."

Cheticamp Field. Designed and hooked by Carol Morris Petillo, Vinalhaven, Maine. 16" by 21".
"Last summer we went to Cheticamp, Nova Scotia to pick up a rug hooking frame I'd ordered. While there, we walked our dogs through a field of wild strawberries, vetch, and star flowers next to our lodging and on the edge of the ocean. This rug is the result of those walks."

Eve, In the Garden of Eden. Designed and hooked by Diane Phillips, Fairport, New York. 51" by 32".
"Eve has taken the blame for so long. I wanted to show her as fully conscious of her options."

Magnolias. Hooked by Sheila M. Breton, Surry, New Hampshire. 14" by 14". Designed by Pearl McGown.

Peace in the Garden. Hooked by Barbara Holt Hussey, Hinsdale, New Hampshire. 46" by 35". Designed by DiFranza Designs.
"I was drawn to this design because of the Peaceable Kingdom nature of it. This was my third rug. The challenge was not so much in its size, but color, as I worked entirely in as-is wool and color planned as I progressed."

Sugar Maple. Designed and hooked by Diane Moore, Morgan, Vermont. 17" by 27".
"Leaves from our front yard dropped on rug backing and, drawn around, were the inspiration for this design."

As Ye Sow. Designed and hooked by Sarah Madison, Amherst, Massachusetts. 32" by 23".
"Besides rug hooking, I also enjoy the hobby of carving in slate, with a special interest in early American gravestone motifs. This rug was inspired by a recent stone carving I completed as a raffle item for a local history museum fundraiser."

Whig Rose. Hooked by Shelley Poremski, Florence, Vermont. 15" diameter. Designed by Nancy Urbanak of Beaver Brook Crafts.

Teapots in the Garden. Designed and hooked by Judith Dallegret, Montreal, Quebec, Canada. 48" by 33".
"This teapot rug was made in memory of a dear, delightful friend, who every summer in Nova Scotia placed her favorite teapots out in her garden in front of her large blooming bushes, a fairyland for teapots."

Folk Art Flower Pots. Designed and hooked by Jeri Laskowski, Rochester, New York. 25" by 26".
"This almost square rug lies in our powder room. The flowers in each pot are folk arty adaptations of the flowers stenciled on the powder room wall. The rug was started as a project in Dick LaBarge's class at Shelburne. I like that any side can be the top of the rug."

Cruzan Garden. Designed and hooked by Sally D'Albora, Rockville, Maryland. 28" by 21".
"Having visited the Caribbean several times, its beauty made a permanent mark in my mind and my heart. In addition to this inspiration, my one brother and his wife have been so kind, and invited us to visit their home on the island of St. Croix, Virgin Islands. This rug is a gift to them."

Seth. Hooked by Maureen Yates, South Burlington, Vermont. 17" by 32". Designed by Stephanie Krauss for Green Mountain Hooked Rugs/Moxley Designs.

A Garden of Flowers, Feathers, and Fur. Hooked by Shirley H. Zandy, Tinmouth, Vermont. 22" by 27". Designed by Tom Zandy.
"My husband has been an avid supporter of my rug hooking, so when I told him I needed a rug with a garden theme, he drew me the arbor and garden rug."

My Favorite Things. Hooked by Beverly J. Delnicki, Wheelock, Vermont. 36" by 48". Designed by Barbara Dawley – Mo Hollow Rugs.
"My friend, Barbara Dawley, designed this rug and was working on it during our group meetings. It was love at first sight and I had to do one for myself."

My Favorite Things. Designed and hooked by Barbara Dawley – Mo Hill Rugs, Newark, Vermont. 36" by 48".
"I designed this rug during a long Vermont winter. Its name, 'My Favorite Things,' says it all. It reflects my love of gardening and the outdoors."

This Was My Garden 2003. Designed and hooked by Susan Alain, Montreal, Quebec, Canada. 32" by 29".
"My garden! And a brown coat I found."

Grandma's Adirondack Garden. Designed and hooked by Helena A. Goldsmith, Plainfield, Vermont. 17" by 15".
"This design was inspired by a little watercolor sketch that my grandmother painted while vacationing in the Adirondacks, as well as my own memories spending time in my other grandmother's garden on Lake George. I dedicate it to them."

Sun Glory. Hooked by Robin Wilson, Ridgefield, Connecticut. 38" by 28". Designed by Michelle Micarelli.

Zen Garden With Pond. Designed and hooked by Gloria Reynolds, Hinesburg, Vermont. 23" by 23".
"My 'want to have' garden."

Prayer Rugs. Designed and hooked by Maddy Fraioli, Roseville, Ohio. 30" by 40" each.
"Shaker inspiration."

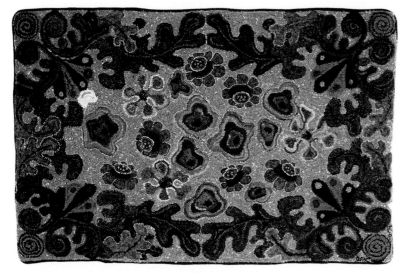

Side Garden/Small Ponds. Designed and hooked by Gloria Reynolds, Hinesburg, Vermont. 13" by 13".
"This 'Side Garden' will work well with 'Zen Garden'. I plan to have both in the future."

Primitive Floral. Designed and hooked by Beverly Conway, Middlebury, Vermont. 56" by 38".

Obdulia. Designed and hooked by Tricia Tague Miller, Alstead, New Hampshire. 45" by 27".
"Friendship is responsible for this rug. Obdulia, a Zapotec Indian whose native dress inspired this design, and Terri Strack, a New England Yankee who dyed the wool for me, made its execution possible."

Three Months of Summer I, II, and III. Designed and hooked by Molly W. Dye, Jacksonville, Vermont. 25" by 19" each.
"My gardens – from ground cover to the tall large sunflowers which feed the birds in the winter. For our very short growing season, I chose to do three separate pieces to capture the fresh first blooms, then next, the midsummer arrivals, finishing with oncoming heartier varieties in their fall attire."

Primrose Path. Hooked by Karen T. Martin, Burlington, Vermont. 34" by 28". Designed by Lib Calloway.

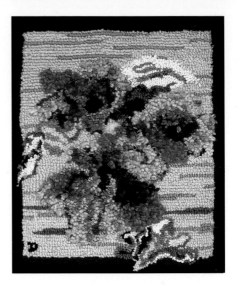

Watercolor Poppies in My Garden. Designed and hooked by Judy B. Dodds, Waitsfield, Vermont. 22" by 18". "Poppies are my favorites! When I learned that the theme of the exhibit was 'In the Garden,' I was inspired to reproduce one of my watercolors. My intent was to take a very different, rather flat and tight medium, and interpret the looseness and flowing quality of watercolor painting. Stand back six feet and you will see."

Folk Art Star. Designed and hooked by Karen Quigley, Vergennes, Vermont. 16" by 16". "A practice project to use colors I don't normally use and to draw my own design."

Home Sweet Home. Designed and hooked by Kathy Devlin, Sunderland, Vermont. 20" by 25". "I decided I'd like to design a rug that would portray the comfort and peace I feel about my home state of Vermont, so I filled it with my favorite things – lily of the valley, oak leaves, and maple trees, a home in the mountains with a new day dawning, a view of heaven on earth. This is my first rug."

Spring. Designed and hooked by Diane Kelly, Dorset, Vermont. 102" by 19". *"Spring is a happiness so beautiful, so unique, so unexpected, that I don't know what to do with my heart."* "These words, written by Emily Dickinson in 1874, inspired this rug. Her poetry captures the joy I feel each spring when we return to Vermont."

Pondlife Triptych: The Fox, The Heron, The Snapping Turtle. Designed and hooked by Peg Irish, Waquoit, Massachusetts. 8" by 8" each.
"Designed for the exhibition entitled 'Crafting From Life' at League of New Hampshire Craftsmen's Foundation Gallery, Concord, New Hampshire. This is an impressionistic view of the garden pond and its visitors in my backyard. It was divided into three parts since the animals do not appear together. The main portion was dyed using a painting technique."

Bennington Flower Basket #1. Designed and hooked by Susan Feller – Ruckman Mill Farm, Augusta, West Virginia. 9" by 12".
"Part 1 of a trilogy – loosely sketched while at Bennington Museum, from blue slip design on stoneware crock, this flower basket has activity and energy in a few simple shapes."

Flower Basket – Abstract #2. Designed and hooked by Susan Feller – Ruckman Mill Farm, Augusta, West Virginia. 9" by 12".
"Part 2 of trilogy – using the same color scheme, I pushed the traditional flower basket design into simpler shapes. The needle felting line of rust was added to increase motion."

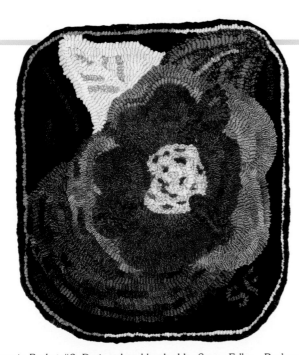

Flower in Basket #3. Designed and hooked by Susan Feller – Ruckman Mill Farm, Augusta, West Virginia. 11" by 10".
"Part 3 of trilogy – closer into the design, this piece has dimension because I sculpted the flower petals and vase. This technique became addicting as I went along – the results are so different with each wool strip."

Through the Knot Hole. Designed and hooked by Kendra B. Curtis, Amsterdam, New York. 33" by 9".
"Watching my chickens in the spring and summer as they run to every bug they see. They are so much fun to watch and I wonder what they are thinking."

Rhus Radicans. Designed and hooked by Linda Rae Coughlin, Warren, New Jersey. 21" by 16". "'Rhus radicans' is the Latin word for poison ivy. This piece is about gossip, where it comes from, and how it will kill you."

Apothecary Rose. Hooked by Kristi Jensen, Schenectady, New York. 48" by 36". Designed by Karen Kahle and Primitive Spirit.

Apothecary Rose. Hooked by Maddy Fraioli, Roseville, Ohio. 48" by 34". Designed by Karen Kahle and Primitive Spirit. "Started in Karen Kahle's spring 2003 class at Shelburne."

Apothecary Rose. Designed and hooked by Karen Kahle and Primitive Spirit, Eugene, Oregon. 48" by 34".
"Influenced by appliqué quilt sampler blocks, I enjoyed hooking each square a little differently than the last. The background simulates the color of old, yellowed muslin."

Chockfull of Posies. Designed and hooked by Linda Repasky, Amherst, Massachusetts. 1.875" by 1.875".
"Miniature punch needle with wool thread."

Tulip Cross. Hooked by Linda Repasky, Amherst, Massachusetts. 2.125" by 2". Design adapted by Linda Repasky from an antique quilt pattern.
"Miniature punch needle used with wool thread."

August Afternoon. Designed and hooked by Rita Barnard, Ann Arbor, Michigan. 44" by 32".
"Every summer my family and I spend a good deal of time in our backyard enjoying the sunshine and gardens. The season always seems too short in Michigan, so by creating this rug we can still enjoy looking at the flowers during the cold winter months."

Iris With Whimsical Border. Designed and hooked by Sara Jane Burghoff, Underhill, Vermont. 35" by 29".
"The garden theme of the rug show this year reminded me of my boyfriend's currently untended garden, which still produces dozens of beautiful irises every year. The whimsical border came about because hearts and swirls are easy and fun to hook. I wanted a spark of color in the corners. Golden stars provided the spark."

Right:
Blue "Flag". Designed and hooked by Cathy Henning, Burlington, Ontario, Canada. 41" by 29".
"For Jane Haliwell's floral workshop I came up with this simple design from a photo of my favorite garden bloom, in a muted stained glass effect. Shading was created using dip-dyed pieces in blues and greens. The background grid was Pro Chem dyes starting with a cool bath to get a mottled effect. The rug is bound with the grid colored wool cut on the bias."

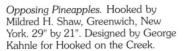

Opposing Pineapples. Hooked by Mildred H. Shaw, Greenwich, New York. 29" by 21". Designed by George Kahnle for Hooked on the Creek.

Pineapple and Flowers. Hooked by Judith English, Cornwall, Vermont. 27" by 19". Designed by Doris Binder for Red Clover Rugs.

Going My Way Iris. Hooked by Susan Andreson, Newport Beach, California. 34" by 23". Designed by Jane Olson.
"I took a photo of my irises in bloom in my garden and Jane Olson drew them for me so I could preserve spring memories forever."

Right:
Fall Arrangement. Designed and hooked by Susan Charbonneau, Kinderhook, New York. 29" by 20".
"A trip to a garden center netted three pumpkins for the front step. Liking the arrangement, I transferred it to a rug."

Pineapple Antique. Hooked by Jill Aiken, Colchester, Vermont. 69" by 35". Designed by Marion Ham – Quail Hill Designs.

Pineapple and Hearts. Hooked by Tom McNerney, Newburyport, Massachusetts. 30" by 30". Designed by Woolen Memories.

Butterfly in My Garden Pillow. Designed and hooked by Karen Baxter Cooper, New London, New Hampshire. 15" by 15".
"Gail Dufresne's class at Shelburne, 2002 inspired this rug. Her inch-mat style was a new concept for me and turned out to be lots of fun to hook. The butterfly coloring came from a book of my mom's and the dip-dyed fabric made it come to life."

71

Bright Wings. Hooked by Susan L. Smidt, Salem, Massachusetts. 60" by 36". Designed by Pearl McGown.
"Bright Wings is one of my early hooked pieces. Ethel Bruce, who was my teacher, taught me about color and dying the swatches for this rug. Keeping the under pattern of flower outlines subtle was a great lesson. I use it to this day."

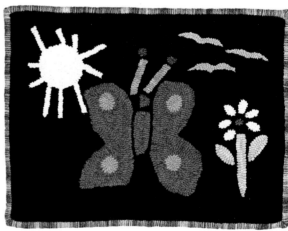

Katherine's Picture. Hooked by Mary Lee O'Connor, Ballston Spa, New York. 20" by 16". Designed by Katherine O'Connor.
"This rug is adapted from a picture my daughter made with her dad when she was about four years old. It is her dad's favorite picture and it has hung in his office for over fourteen years."

Left:
Sampler Flowers. Hooked by Lisa Mims, Flemington, New Jersey. 18" by 24". Designed by Susan Feller – Ruckman Mill Farm.
"The colors for this rug came from scrap bags and were chosen with the help of many of my friends! My seven-year-old daughter, Lexi, hooked one of the flowers. At the 2003 Cortina hook-in, Susan took pity on my slow hooking style and helped me work on the background."

72

Primitive Poppies. Hooked by Laura Podob, Farmington Hills, Michigan. 45" by 24". Design adapted from the folk art of Millie Shaw by Kris Miller and Spruce Ridge Studios.

Primitive Poppies. Hooked by Terri Cronin, Norwalk, Connecticut. 48" by 23". Design adapted from the folk art of Millie Shaw by Kris Miller and Spruce Ridge Studios.

Primitive Poppies. Hooked by Rita Barnard, Ann Arbor, Michigan. 45" by 24". Design adapted from the folk art of Millie Shaw by Kris Miller and Spruce Ridge Studios.

Star Flower. Designed and hooked by Judy Quintman, Wilmington, North Carolina. 34" by 29".
"I was doodling one day and drew some stars and circles, and suddenly they were in a pot. It was fun to take the shapes of the flowers and move them out to the border."

Right:
Flowers and Stars. Hooked by Jeri Laskowski, Rochester, New York. 26" by 34". Design adapted from the folk art of Millie Shaw by Kris Miller and Spruce Ridge Studios.
"This basket of fantasy flowers and its penny rug suggestion is my favorite rug – well at least it's in the top three favorites."

American Historic. Hooked by Tina Payton, Mexico, Maine. 32" by 43". Designed by Marion Ham – Quail Hill Designs.

Vase of Flowers. Designed and hooked by Nancy Ellingham, Batavia, New York. 34" by 24". "I wanted to do a rug with big flowers and bright colors."

Right:
Antique Floral. Designed and hooked by Nancy L. Taylor, Gorham, Maine. 40" by 32".
"I have a pewter bowl in my kitchen that I used as the basis for this design. I had always wanted to learn fine shading, so with my teacher's help (Jackye Hansen), this rug was created."

Lavender Basket. Hooked by Cindy House, Hinesburg, Vermont. 36" by 29". Designed by Karen Kahle and Primitive Spirit.

Untitled #2. Designed and hooked by Lucinda Seward, Pittsford, Vermont. 28" by 57".
"This rug was inspired by the border on an early quilt in the Henry Ford Museum in Dearborn, Michigan."

Sentimental. Designed and hooked by Karen Kahle and Primitive Spirit, Eugene, Oregon. 38" by 26".
"A friend suggested that I create a new floral design using motifs from some of my other rugs, Moss Rose and Peony. As it turned out, I designed two rugs. This was my favorite of the two, which I hooked, and my friend hooked the other (her favorite, lucky for me!) called Peony and Roses."

Bed Rug With Floral Design. Designed and hooked by Susan Gault, Thetford Center, Vermont. 90" by 72".
"The inspiration for this rug came from American Bed Rugs made in the late 18th and early 19th centuries. Typically, the designs of these rugs were bold, naive, and free. They were either hooked or yarn sewn. The word 'rug' originally indicated a bed covering and only later referred to floor covering."

Flower Basket. Hooked by Nancy Urbanak, Cornwall, Vermont. 31" by 21".
Design adapted from an early 20th century wall hanging.
"I found this design in *Hooked Rugs, an American Folk Art,* by Leslie Linsley. I
have wanted to hook this pattern for years. I overdyed red plaids for the
background and hooked it horizontally."

Shelburne Souvenir. Designed and hooked by Lory Doolittle,
Mt. Holly, Vermont. 39" by 35".
"This rug was inspired by a class given by Jule Marie Smith. We
were encouraged to use designs found on items in the museum.
Bev Conway encouraged the colors for the flowers."

Strong House Fire Board Adaptation. Designed and hooked by Lory
Doolittle, Mt. Holly, Vermont. 27" by 27". Upholstered by Shoreham
Upholstery.
"This design was adapted from a fire board in the John Strong,
D.A.R. (Daughters of the American Revolution) House in West
Addison, Vermont."

Spring. Hooked by Yvonne Isabelle, Williamstown,
Vermont. 36" by 22". Designed by Anne Ashworth.
"This is only my second rug."

Norma's Garden Bouquet. Hooked by Tom McNerney,
Newburyport, Massachusetts. 24" by 38". Designed by
Tom McNerney and Gull Cottage Rugs.
"My inspiration for this design of a primitive pot of flowers
came from the floral bouquets of Norma Graf, a member
of the West Newbury Rug Guild and an avid gardener."

A William Morris Tulip for Mary Beth. Hooked by Jeri Laskowski, Rochester, New York. 14" by 14".
"This will be a pillow cover for my daughter-in-law, Mary Beth. She is a pattern design artist and is fond of William Morris tapestries. My husband Leo drew this adaptation of one of William Morris' tulip motifs."

Potted Garden. Hooked by Karen Baxter Cooper, New London, New Hampshire. 36" by 34". Design adapted by Karen Baxter Cooper from an antique rug.

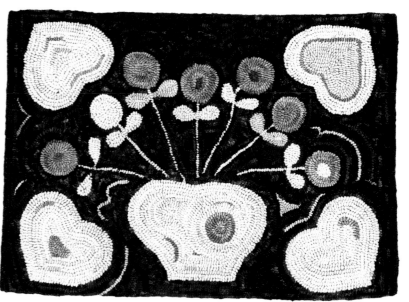

Urn with Flowers. Hooked by Dee Wagner, Brookfield, Connecticut. 18" by 26". Designer unknown.
"I found a photo of this antique rug in one of my favorite books: *Seasons at Seven Gates Farm*, the home of James Cramer and Dean Johnson. I used a brown and black plaid for the background and wools dyed by Marilyn Bottjer."

Shelburne, Vermont - "Tulips and Others". Hooked by Stephanie A. Krauss, Montpelier, Vermont. 18" by 24". Designed by Susan Feller – Ruckman Mill Farm.
"This particular design caught my eye when I was a vendor at the Shelburne Show in 2003. I thought it might be fun to get a piece of wool from each of the vendors at the show that year and hook each piece into the rug as a memento. I chose lots of colors that I liked, but didn't decide on the color plan until I got home after the show."

Chapter 5

Animals

Oxen in Summer. Hooked by Tricia Tague Miller, Alstead, New Hampshire. 19" by 19". Designed by Maud Lewis.
"I needed a piece to decrease my pile of leftovers from previous projects. This was a delightful choice!"

Maple. Designed and hooked by Janet Knight, Lebanon, New Hampshire. 17" by 14".
"The inspiration for this rug was a picture of the face of a jersey cow with a maple leaf in her mouth. I depicted the cow as if she were peering out of a small barn window, with a maple tree branch within her reach. The border is shades of gray to represent a barn board frame with a small gold inset."

Eight in One. Hooked by Cathy Henning, Burlington, Ontario, Canada. 39" by 46". Designed by Cathy Henning with birdhouse drawn courtesy of George Kahnle.
"For Dick LaBarge and George Kahnle's Primitive Workshop, I used as many of my 'rug to be' ideas as I could to make one unified piece. My experimental marbleizing provided the brighter than normal color pallet. The two together produced this rug. I used two border treatments to avoid my usual mirror-image effect and concealed the date and my initials in the lower border. It was good to get eight rugs hooked and finished!"

The Fox Went Out. Designed and hooked by Sally W. Kirouac, Saratoga Springs, New York. 41" by 59".
"Based on the anonymous folk song 'The Fox Went Out on a Chilly Night,' sung by Burl Ives and Odetta."

Three's Company. Hooked and adapted by Susan Lathrop, Cambridgeport, Vermont. 23" by 22".
"Inspired by a notepad design by Polly Holabird (d.b.a. Polly Prodie). Color and technique advice by Jan Seavey."

Lily's Rug. Hooked by Rebecca Erb, Sinking Spring, Pennsylvania. 31" by 18". Designed by Rebecca Erb and Matt Moore.
"A nursery rug for our granddaughter, incorporating lots of fun colors and her yellow lab, Molly."

Cow On Acid. Designed and hooked by Joelle Hochman, Somerville, Massachusetts. 14" by 12".
"Second in a series of animal mats. I decided to work with the colors not typically in my palette. My husband says it looks like I was on drugs when I made it…hence the name!"

Dancin' Hams. Hooked by Tony Latham, Montreal, Quebec, Canada. 28" by 24". Designed by Jessica Hughes for Primco.

Giraffe. Designed and hooked by Diane S. Learmonth, Newton, Iowa. 28" by 20". "This giraffe lives and breathes at Binder Park Zoo in Battle Creek, Michigan. My husband took this photo while we were standing in the exhibit, hand-feeding the giraffe. I had to hook him – he's beautiful."

Charging Elephant. Hooked by Jon Ciemiewicz, Litchfield, New Hampshire. 24" by 24". Design adapted by Jon Ciemiewicz from an original picture by Steve Bloom Images. "A photograph found on the web by Steve Bloom is the source of this design. Steve captured his original picture in late day sunlight conditions, which provided the light dark contrast that I tried to capture in the rug."

Blue Moose. Designed and hooked by Jon Ciemiewicz, Litchfield, New Hampshire. 24" by 30".
"This rug was designed from a composite of several public domain images found on the World Wide Web. In all of the images, the moose was lying down – a plus because I did not have to try to incorporate a set of gangly legs."

Fall Harvest. Designed and hooked by Karen Detrick, New Lexington, Ohio. 46" by 35".
"My husband requested a large realistic turkey rug for our entryway. Watching and photographing the real thing outside in our front yard gave me all the reference materials I needed. Color planning the background and border coordinated with the interior of our home."

Proud Turkey/Prodded Turkey. Designed and hooked by Janet Williams, Skillman, New Jersey. 27" by 35".
"I have always wanted to do a Thanksgiving turkey; these are beautiful birds that project an American theme, a patriotic theme."

The Vermont Turkey. Hooked by Debbie Kirby, Brandon, Vermont. 39" by 32". Designed by Warren Kimble.
"Warren drew the turkey on the monk's cloth and I did the dyeing and hooking. All the mohair in the yarn used is from the goats on my farm. The rug will be donated to the Brandon Artists' Guild for their silent auction in conjunction with the 'Brandon is for the Birds' fund raiser."

Old Chalk Deer. Hooked by Tricia Tague Miller, Alstead, New Hampshire. 35" by 28". Designed by Edyth O'Neill.
"Through Edyth's web site this pattern was found. My challenge was to execute the figures using only recycled wools from old clothing. Goal achieved."

Midnight at the Garden Pool. Hooked by Edith McClure, Farmington, Connecticut. 33" by 20". Designed by Beverly Conway Designs.
"I decided to use the bright colors I had dyed to create an unusual effect."

Band Box Squirrels. Hooked by Dorothy Panaceck, Fredricksburg, Texas. 19" by 30". Designed by Edyth O'Neill.
"Edyth is a dear friend and I loved the pattern. I like to add unspun wool into my rugs and used llama wool in their tails for texture."

Farmyard Geese. Hooked by Tricia Tague Miller, Alstead, New Hampshire. 21" by 27". Designed by Joan Moshimer.
"Inspired by an old *Rug Hookers News & Views* magazine."

Skunk and Skunk Border. Hooked by Judith English, Cornwall, Vermont. 36" by 24". Design adapted by Red Clover Rugs from an antique hooked rug.

Foxy. Hooked by Cecelia K. Toth, West Arlington, Vermont. 40" by 24". Designed by Cynthia McAdoo of McAdoo Rugs.

Right:
Animal Tapestry. Hooked by Tricia Tague Miller, Alstead, New Hampshire. 24" by 20". Designed by DiFranza Designs.
"When I was a child, Easter often meant a visit to The Cloisters in New York City to tour the gardens and medieval tapestries. The sight of this pattern brought back those memories – and how I love to hook animals! Trying to give the impression of a weaving, I intentionally dyed and hooked some areas to look a bit streaky and vertical. Would you guess the background is Black Watch plaid?"

A Moose for Janet. Designed and hooked by Carolyn Barney, Canaan, New Hampshire. 24" by 18".
"Our daughter, Janet, after years of vacationing and camping in New England, has yet to see a moose in the wild. So, when I was looking for a theme for my next rug, she requested a moose. This consolation moose was designed and created for the family room in her log cabin home."

Peaceable Kingdom. Hooked by Johanna White, Hinesburg, Vermont. 46" by 32". Designed by Patsy Becker.

Dinosaurs for Grandkids. Designed and hooked by Alan S. Kidder, Rochester, Vermont. 41" by 15".
"Two preschool grandchildren love dinosaurs. 'Grandpa, make me a rug with a blue dinosaur.' Scientists now think dinosaurs were brightly colored like the Gila monster. So two boys got their wish – mod-colored dinosaurs."

Parade of Animals. Hooked by Pamela Carter, Bristol, Vermont. 80" by 18". Designed by Woolen Memories.

Author's note: In order to make the rug show more interesting for young people, we decided to have a "children's challenge." A sign with a photograph of the hen found in "Parade of Animals" greeted youngsters at the entry with the question, "Can you find this chicken? She is hidden somewhere in one of the rugs. Find her and win a prize." There was great excitement each time the chicken was spotted and we quickly had to replenish our basket of prizes. I asked several kids if they thought the chicken was hard to find and they all answered, "No." This was especially interesting to me because on opening night I realized that the volunteers had hung all the rugs and I had no idea where the chicken was. I asked four different adults to find the chicken so we would know where she was for the challenge. Not one of the grown-ups could meet the chicken challenge. Special thanks to Pamela Carter for hooking this feathered star of the show that made so many children happy.

Animals. Designed and hooked by Lucinda Seward, Pittsford, Vermont. 26" by 46".

Top Heavy. Hooked by Rebecca Erb, Sinking Spring, Pennsylvania. 42" by 21". Designed by Vermont Folk Rugs.

Playing Leap Fox. Designed and hooked by Linda Repasky, Amherst, Massachusetts. 24" by 19".

Moose, Raccoon, Bat, Turtle, Cat, Rooster, Fox, and Skunk – Stair Risers. Hooked by Julie Rogers, Huntington, Vermont. 25" by 6" each. Designed by Evelyn Lawrence for Beverly Conway Designs.

Skinny Cow. Hooked by Diana M. Link, Danby, Vermont. 24" by 5". Designed by Evelyn Lawrence for Beverly Conway Designs.

Running Rooster. Hooked by Diana M. Link, Danby, Vermont. 24" by 5".
Designed by Evelyn Lawrence for Beverly Conway Designs.

Golden Retriever. Hooked by Deb Kelley, Shoreham, Vermont. 6" by 24". Designed by Evelyn Lawrence for Beverly Conway Designs.

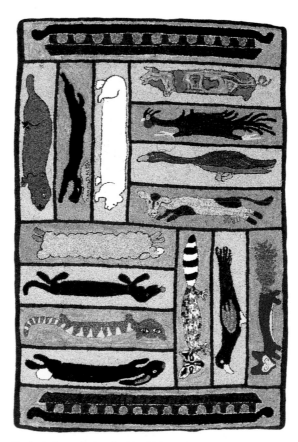

Evelyn's Animals. Hooked by Melonie Bushey, Vergennes, Vermont. 48" by 60". Designed by Evelyn Lawrence and Beverly Conway for Beverly Conway Designs.

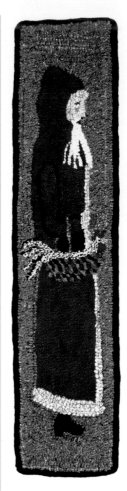

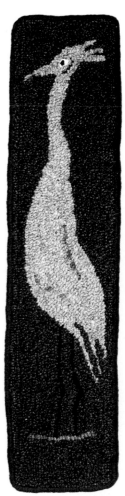

Great Blue Heron. Hooked by Karen Quigley, Vergennes, Vermont. 28" by 9". Designed by Evelyn Lawrence for Beverly Conway Designs.
"I once had the prehistoric heron living in my backyard. His elegance and simplicity led to replication in wool."

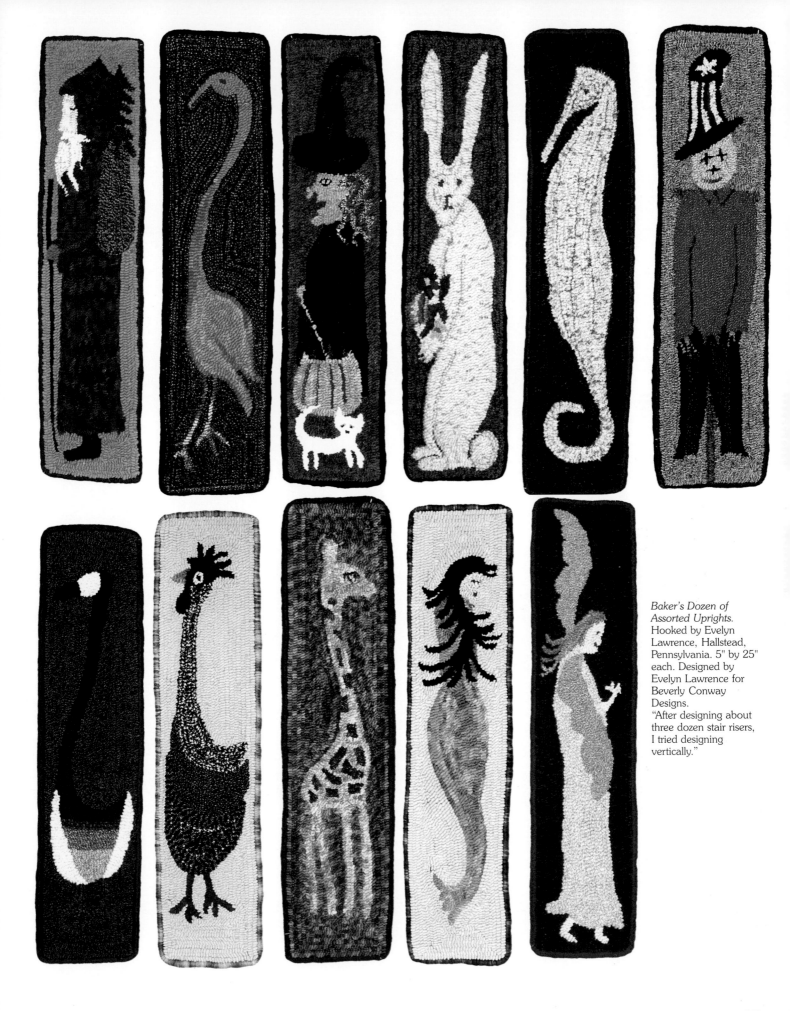

Baker's Dozen of Assorted Uprights. Hooked by Evelyn Lawrence, Hallstead, Pennsylvania. 5" by 25" each. Designed by Evelyn Lawrence for Beverly Conway Designs.
"After designing about three dozen stair risers, I tried designing vertically."

Antique Lion. Designed and hooked by Karen Kahle and Primitive Spirit, Eugene, Oregon. 51" by 26".
"Last year in Amy Oxford's class, I saw one of Shelburne Museum's antique rugs of a tiger. Its charm inspired me to design this lion, adapted from a sketch of a Heraldic Lion. Gentle and quaint, I wanted him to look like he was drawn by someone who had never seen a lion."

Klee's Cat. Designed and hooked by Debra Boudrieau, Bellows Falls, Vermont. 35" by 18".
"I have loved the artist Paul Klee since college. His use of light and dark, shape, and superimposed images inspired me to design this rug in a geometric class taught by Gail Dufresne."

Dream Kitty. Designed and hooked by Lisa Mims, Flemington, New Jersey. 27" by 24".

"Dream Kitty began in Rae Harrell's Balancing Act class at Shelburne in 2002. After college I moved to Atlanta and adopted twin orange kitties, Ted and George. They were my trusty companions for twelve years. I always wanted to hook a big orange cat rug in their honor. My daughter Lexi added the heart. My family ate a lot of take-out in order for me to make the show deadline!"

Kittens on the Deck. Designed and hooked by Marion Collins, South Burlington, Vermont. 30" by 27".

"This is my own design of my granddaughter's deck, where her cats like to play and sleep in the sun."

Sabrina and the Potted Flowers. Designed and hooked by Susan DeGregorio, Salem, New Hampshire. 25" by 32".

"The folk art cat is modeled after my black Persian, Sabrina. I say 'folk art' because Sabrina's tail is actually fuller. However, she does have the many browns, blacks, grays, and reddish-browns that are under her chin and on her chest. I also took the liberty of leaving some raised wool loops to give an added dimension to the cat's fur and pot's rim. Her eyes and her posture are set as if she is ready to say, 'I am sitting here for what? And when do I get my treat?'"

Porcelain Cat. Designed and hooked by Sue Hammond, New London, New Hampshire. 36" by 24".

"This was inspired by a blue porcelain cat and surrounded with cat paws for the fun of it."

Lion. Hooked by Judith B. Bush, Woodstock, Vermont. 24" by 38". Designer unknown. "I found this in a book purchased at a used book store. The original was a yarn sewn rug, c.1850, maker unknown. The info is from *Folk Art in American Life*, by Robert Bishop and Jacqueline M. Atkins, published by Viking Studio Books.

Primitive Cat. Hooked by Karen Quigley, Vergennes, Vermont. 14" by 11". Designed by Woolen Memories. "Primitive cat, rag look – appeals to me as a basic project with an 'old' look."

Kats Pajamas. Designed and hooked by Lindsay Millen, Boxford, Massachusetts. 17" by 23". "My first rug." Lindsay Millen, age fifteen.

Cat in the Garden. Designed and hooked by Jacqueline L. Hansen of Jacqueline Hansen Designs, Scarborough, Maine. 38" by 24".
"This is a hooking of my cat, a 'Black Bombay' named Amos. He is sixteen years young and sits like this in my garden, which I can view from my kitchen window. He was the inspiration for this design. I 'hoved' the flowers to give it dimension in the Waldoboro technique: raised and sheared."

Right:
Just a Cat Mat. Hooked by Karen Quigley, Vergennes, Vermont. 18" by 14". Designed by Moondance Color Company.
"Again, my love of animals and gardening combined with the bright colors of spring."

Freddie Footstool. Designed and hooked by Lory Doolittle, Mt. Holly, Vermont. 14" diameter. Upholstered by Shoreham Upholstery.
"This footstool is the result of a class by Elizabeth Black."

Cat's in the Bag. Designed and hooked by Linda Repasky, Amherst, Massachusetts. 13" by 10".

Orange Cat. Designed and hooked by Linda Repasky, Amherst, Massachusetts. 21" by 16".

Fat Cat #199 in my Catalog. Designed and hooked by Patsy Becker, South Orleans, Massachusetts. 27" by 30".
"A student at Green Mountain Rug School requested a cat design – 'Fat Cat' was born. Since the pattern was added to my catalog, at least a hundred hookers have made him their own. I too had to challenge myself, using many sizes of handcuts and numerous yellows to make my fat cat happy."

Fat Cat. Hooked by Patti Varley, Saratoga Springs, New York. 30" by 27". Designed by Patsy Becker.
"Reminded me of a beloved cat that was a family member for twelve years."

"Fat Cat" Choco in the Garden. Hooked by Jill Aiken, Colchester, Vermont. 28" by 25". Designed by Patsy Becker.

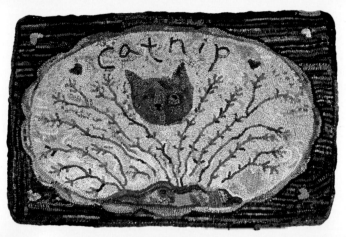

Catnip. Designed and hooked by Karen Kahle and Primitive Spirit, Eugene, Oregon. 33" by 21".
"As an herb gardener and cat lover, I planted catnip below my roses only to make fast friends with Simple, the neighbor's cat. I caught her drunk and in love next to her favorite herb, and knew that I would somehow have to capture the scene in a rug. I was pleased at how my design caught the moment."

Max. Designed and hooked by Linda Repasky, Amherst, Massachusetts. 23" by 19".

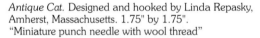

Antique Cat. Designed and hooked by Linda Repasky, Amherst, Massachusetts. 1.75" by 1.75".
"Miniature punch needle with wool thread"

Princeton Tigers. Designed and hooked by Pandy Goodbody, Williamstown, Massachusetts. 45" by 31".
"This Princeton jungle scene was inspired by Henri Rousseau. The rug will be in a fall 2004 show sponsored by the Tiger Ladies of Princeton (otherwise known as the Mercer Rug Hookers). It will be for sale at that show."

Friendly Cat. Hooked by Susan Gingras, Weybridge, Vermont. 40" tall. Designed by Beverly Conway Designs.
"A cat that doesn't scratch the couch – perfect!"

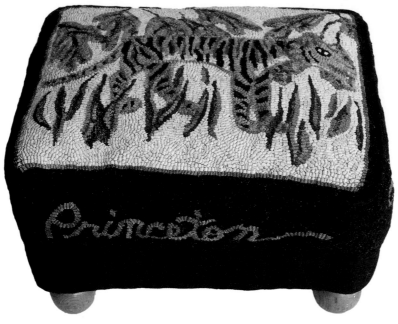

Tiger. Designed and hooked by Roberta Smith, West Windsor, New Jersey. 19" diameter.

Princeton Tiger Stool. Designed and hooked by Claudia Casebolt, Lawrenceville, New Jersey. 14" by 18" by 10".
"This stool was designed as one of the 'Tiger Rugs' to go in an exhibit in October, 2004 by the 'Tiger Ladies' of Princeton."

Tigers in Paradise. Hooked by Theresa Strack, Bedford, New Hampshire. 36" by 64". Designed by Elizabeth Black and Terri Strack.
"I have always loved the beauty and majesty of the rare white tigers. Elizabeth and I had discussed at length what I wanted to incorporate into my next challenge. This rug is the completed result of a wonderful collaboration."

Flat Cat. Hooked by Kathie Barbour, Hanover, New Hampshire. 38" by 26". Designed by Leslie Barbour when she was eight years old.
"My daughter, Leslie, did a painting of 'flat cat' when she was in third grade in Ann Arbor, Michigan. I have always loved this cheerful image and hooked the piece for her."

Content. Designed and hooked by DonnaSue Shaw, Grand Isle, Vermont. 22" by 12".
"I designed this rug in honor of the many blessings that fill my every day."

Gizmo. Designed and hooked by Becky Behrendt, Schenectady, New York. 21" by 31".

Cat Love. Designed and hooked by Burma Cassidy, Rochester, Vermont. 15" by 15".
"This stool cover brings the joy of this sweet cat, filled with a rainbow of love."

Cat and Mouse. Hooked by Julie Rogers, Huntington, Vermont. 27" by 22". Designed by Karen Kahle and Primitive Spirit.

Warren Kimble's Checkerboard Cats. Hooked by Dot Danforth, Arlington, Vermont. 27" by 18". Designed by Warren Kimble.
"This rug was inspired by Warren Kimble's 2004 'Cats' calendar."

Cats and Birds. Designed and hooked by Lucinda Seward, Pittsford, Vermont. 34" by 21".

Dogs

Lucy in the Sky with Diamonds. Designed and hooked by Gail Ferdinando, Pittstown, New Jersey. 30" by 21".
"This is the first time I designed my own rug, which was created in Dick and George's Dye and Design class. Of course, it had to include my new puppy, Lucy."

Gaia – Party Animal. Designed and hooked by Suzi Prather, Orlando, Florida. 23" by 20".
"This is my first fine cut realistic-looking rug. I took a class from Elizabeth Black to be able to hook this for my son. Gaia is his dog and always ready for fun."

Katie. Hooked by Norma Graf, West Newbury, Massachusetts. 38" by 26". Design modified by Norma Graf from the pattern 'The Hunt' by Marion Ham – Quail Hill Designs.
Katie was my dog for fifteen years. She passed away this winter. She was a 'sweetheart' with a real 'heart' on her coat. Katie was a very special dog inside and out.

Abby Watches Her Sheep. Hooked by Nancy Phillips, North Fayston, Vermont. 46" by 33". Designed by Marion Ham - Quail Hill Designs.
"I raise sheep and train border collies. Each of my dogs has been hooked on a rug. This old Kopp hooked rug (from the book *American Hooked and Sewn Rugs: Folk Art Underfoot*, by Joel and Kate Kopp) catches the essence of my dog Abby. She's a very keen dog."

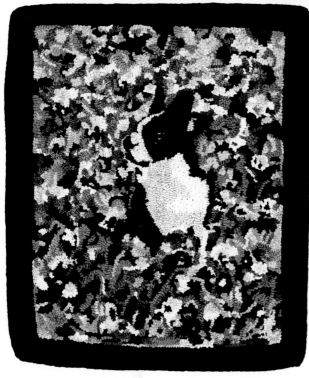

Gus in Bluebonnets. Designed and hooked by Shelley Poremski, Florence, Vermont. 24" by 20".
"I hooked this picture of Gus, my daughter Courtney's Boston Terrier, sitting in a field of bluebonnets. It was my first rug and I hooked it using Amy Oxford's punch hook method and The Oxford Punch Needle."

It's Our Dog's Life. Designed and hooked by Beth McDermet, Salem, Massachusetts. 32" by 26".
"This is a composite of our three wonderful dogs – Cleo and Maggie (both deceased) and our two-year-old, Sophie. The dog is surrounded by their favorite toys in the scalloped frame. And what black lab is happy without water, frogs, squirrels and (unfortunately) skunks to chase? They all loved their daily walks, so the leash is lying in wait."

Homeward Bound. Hooked and adapted from an antique rug by Rachel T. Jacobs, Montpelier, Vermont. 51" by 26".
"The inspiration to hook this impressionistic primitive was influenced by a surplus of mostly green cut strips. No attention was given to scale or perspective. The dogs, cattle, sheep, and geese are all a part of my life growing up in rural Vermont."

Verve. Designed and hooked by Tricia Tague Miller, Alstead, New Hampshire. 18" by 16".
"It was love at first sight between me and my boy, Verve! An opportunity to study under Elizabeth Black encouraged me to attempt his portrait. A photo was blown up and further enlarged by my using a projector and tracing the image. Terri Strack provided the wool and this is the result of an intense three day effort. I'm happy!"

Black is the Color of My True Love's Nose. Designed and hooked by Jen Lavoie, Huntington, Vermont. 27" by 44".

ABBEY'S FOLK ARK

Abbey's Folk Ark. Designed and hooked by Suzi Prather, Orlando, Florida. 46" by 27".
"I had been wanting to do another rug of my dog when I was challenged to do a Noah's Ark Rug. My most unusual mind came up with the idea of my brilliant dog seeing a storm coming and wanting to get my folk art ark into the water before the flood came."

Australian Shepherd. Designed and hooked by Marilyn L. Sly, Mystic, Connecticut. 19" by 25".

Balls and Bones. Hooked by Susan Gingras, Weybridge, Vermont. 37" by 19". Designed by Beverly Conway Designs.
"This was the perfect rug to hook for my sister! She has a pack of five little dogs!"

Clyde. Hooked by Melonie Bushey, Vergennes, Vermont. Designed by Beverly Conway Designs. 37" tall, by 19" wide, by 9" deep.

Lucifer's Piano Bench. Designed and hooked by Amy Oxford, Cornwall, Vermont. 38" by 18" by 18". Upholstered by Shoreham Upholstery.
"This bench originally belonged to my great-grandmother and was covered with a beautiful floral needlepoint design that she made. Decades later, when the needlepoint began to wear out, my father asked if I would reupholster it for him with a picture of his dog, Lucifer, who went by the much cozier name of 'Furry'. Furry, a bouvier, belonged to my dad, John Soutter, and also to my sister, Lucy Soutter. Furry's favorite thing to do was to jump in the pool, go for a long swim, and then roll around happily in our ivy patch. She loved this so much that when she died, her ashes were sprinkled on the ivy. In spite of her name, she was a very good dog."

99

Fish

Sacred Fish. Designed and hooked by Burma Cassidy, Rochester, Vermont. 30" by 33".

"Sacred fish was inspired by my travels to Three Rivers Petroglyph Site in New Mexico. I captured the geometric landscape surrounding this unusual drawing found amongst the desert rocks."

Pez Gato (Cat Fish). Hooked by Rosario Villavicencio, Mamaroneck, New York. 49" by 21". Design adapted from the folk art of Millie Shaw by Kris Miller and Spruce Ridge Studios.

"I have cats at home and like to observe them when I'm hooking. They're always interesting and elegant. They'd sit by the sea, basking in the sun, if they'd had a fish tail. Rich colors, high contrasts, they define Pez Gato well."

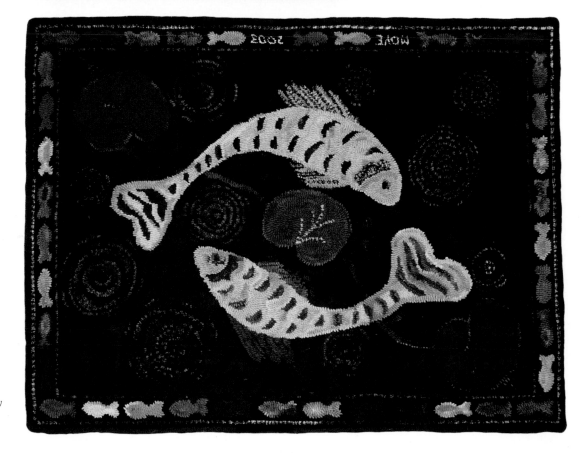

Fish Pond. Hooked by Molly W. Dye, Jacksonville, Vermont. 30" by 23". Designed by Charco.

Fish and Friends. Hooked by Diana O'Brien, Shelburne, Massachusetts. 33" by 22". Designed by Liz O'Brien of Liziana Creations.

She is a Salmon. Designed and hooked by Bonnie Olson, Rutland, Vermont. 38" by 47".
"Atlantic salmon fishing in New Brunswick each September is an inspiring adventure. The salmon hatch in streams and swim out to sea to Greenland, return to their stream to spawn the next generation, and die. My rug is a tribute to this strong fish and my imagining of what the view from beneath the water's surface is like. This rug represents a female salmon; the male would have a longer, hooked lower jaw which develops once it returns to the stream."

Fish and Friends. Hooked by Sherry Craig Lowe, Glastonbury, Connecticut. 26" by 36". Designed by Liziana Creations.
"I grew up on Nantucket Island and have always loved the ocean. I was challenged, as a punch needle rug hooker, to demonstrate shading. I used sixteen separate colors of blue, 100% wool, 3-ply yarn to hook the ocean."

Shells. Hooked by Diana O'Brien, Shelburne, Massachusetts. 30" by 24". Designed by Liz O'Brien of Liziana Creations.

Long Fish. Designed and hooked by Miriam Henning, Truro, Massachusetts. 6" by 24".
"The source for this design is my imagination."

Shelburne Shapes and Whales. Hooked by Dayne Sousa, Pinehurst, North Carolina. 27" by 38". Designed by Jule Marie Smith and Dayne Sousa.
"I developed this rug in a class with Jule Marie Smith's guidance in 2002 after visiting some restored houses in the museum."

View from the Nautilus. Designed and hooked by Louise Scott, Tinmouth, Vermont. 37" by 50".

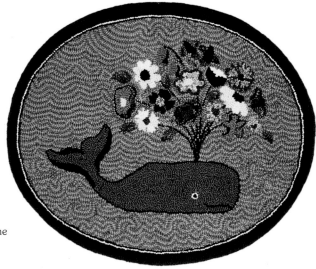

Whale Spouting Flowers. Hooked by Sherry Craig Lowe, Glastonbury, Connecticut. 28" by 33". Designed by The George Wells Ruggery.
"I grew up on Nantucket Island and have always loved and been fascinated by whales. I was curious to see if I could show movement in the water using a punch needle and four separate colors of wool yarn."

Three Little Fishes. Designed and hooked by Miriam Henning, Truro, Massachusetts. 6" by 24".

Birds

The Gossips. Hooked by Cecelia Toth, West Arlington, Vermont. 36" by 24". Designed by Marion Ham - Quail Hill Designs.

Kallie's Kaw. Designed and hooked by Kathy Hutchins, Chittenden, Vermont. 17" by 15".
"In memory of Kallie Belle, my chocolate lab."

Pumpkin Pickin'. Hooked by Trish Becker, The Woolery, Inc., Lebanon, New Jersey. 48" by 32". Designed by Trish Becker with art by Sherri Hieber Day. *Copyright Art Interests 2003.*
"Inspired by visits to my twin's Maine garden, picking pumpkins on a blistery October day amid falling leaves and calling crows. It was a joy for me to color plan and dye the wool with my own original color formulas. I loved shading the pumpkin and hooking the iridescent crows. This is my second rug. Original design and message by me. Art by Sherri Hieber Day."

Peafowl, Willow, and Cedars. Designed and hooked by Barbara Kaiser, Cornwall, Vermont. 37" by 25".
"I have had peafowl for many years and they love to spend time under the willow tree and cedar trees in my yard. I spend many hours watching them. Their colors, sounds, textures, and peacefulness inspired me to hook this rug."

Glorious Sunflower. Hooked by Davey DeGraff, Hinesburg, Vermont. 55" by 20". Design adapted from the folk art of Millie Shaw by Kris Miller and Spruce Ridge Studios.

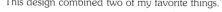

Sunflower and Crows. Hooked by Susan Gingras, Weybridge, Vermont. 55" by 21". Design adapted from the folk art of Millie Shaw by Kris Miller and Spruce Ridge Studios.
"This design combined two of my favorite things."

My Brother's Crow. Designed and hooked by DonnaSue Shaw, Grand Isle, Vermont. 24" by 20". "I wanted to create a masculine rug with an unusual border. I had a lot of fun playing with fabrics, techniques, and color."

The Crow for P. Pie. Hooked by Kris McDermet, Dummerston, Vermont. 34" by 38". Designed by Jeanne Benjamin, border by Kris McDermet. "I love crows! Jeanne Benjamin's pattern is so beautiful and I added the penny rug tongues and braided border. Our wonderful golden dog, Luke, died as I was finishing this. We called him P. Pie. He spent many hours at my feet while I hooked."

Right:
Come Live with Me. Designed and hooked by Cheryl Dulong-Wasielewski, Greenfield, Massachusetts. 36" by 24".
"I made this rug for two wonderful neighbors, Mike and Karen Little, who are also very gifted artists who appreciate everything that goes into one's work. The Crow (Mike) is giving the Queen Bee (Karen) a rose and asking her to 'come live with me…' Mike is an entrepreneur and Karen raises bees."

Below:
Autumn Friends. Designed and hooked by Susan Feller – Ruckman Mill Farm, Augusta, West Virginia. 29" by 53".
"Large geometric shapes with multiple borders framing three simple birds are reminiscent of antique rugs. This rug was colored after hearing Barb Carroll describe her textures and repeat borders approach to primitive designs."

Cardinal Rules. Designed and hooked by Gwenn C. Smith, Lebanon, New Hampshire. 18" by 12". "The beauty of cardinals against a winter sky in a snowstorm. A delight!"

105

On the Wing. Hooked by Sandi Reiber, Chittenden, Vermont. 32" by 36". Designed by Pearl McGown Collection.

"This is a Pearl McGown design on burlap I bought at an auction. I transferred it onto linen and added the mountains to make it 'Vermont Geese On the Wing.' The original burlap pattern had a Chinese stamp on it."

Tern Unstoned. Designed and hooked by Mary Guay, Grand Isle, Vermont. 23" by 35".

"I visited Florida in November 2003 and was fascinated with royal terns running in flocks on Nokomis Beach. I saw them again in Costa Rica! The title of the rug is 'Tern Unstoned' after a joke told to me about terns. This was my first big rug."

Mottled Duck. Hooked by Jon Ciemiewicz, Litchfield, New Hampshire. 18" by 24". Design adapted by Jon Ciemiewicz.

"The inspiration for this design is Adam Grimm's painting that was chosen as the 2000 Federal Duck Stamp. I was immediately attracted to the backlighting that Adam captured in his image. However, in doing the adaptation I added a sunset sky that was not in Adam's original picture."

Fowl Play. Designed and hooked by Shirley Chaiken, Lebanon, New Hampshire. 30" by 31".

"I came across an old piecework pamphlet and saw a teardrop-shaped bird. I couldn't resist using that shape to make this rug."

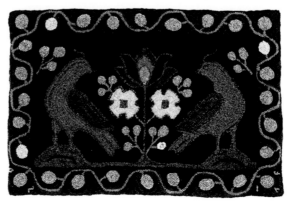

Ohio Coverlet. Hooked by Lucille B. Festa, Wilton, Connecticut. 36" by 26". Designed by Edith O'Neill.

Black Bird. Designed, hooked, and braided by Milda Peake, Brattleboro, Vermont. 13" diameter.
"I like the Black Bird! I like to watch them, they are so interesting and smart."

Bird on the Vine. Hooked by Jean Brana, South Burlington, Vermont. 18" by 26". Designed by DiFranza Designs.

Almond Blossoms. Hooked by Kathy Gage, South Burlington, Vermont. 15" by 19". Designed by Karen Kahle and Primitive Spirit.

Almond Blossoms. Hooked by Sharon Laufer, Williamstown, Vermont. 19" by 15". Designed by Karen Kahle and Primitive Spirit.
"In our Vermont garden, we see bluebirds and goldfinches. This design by Primitive Spirit reminds me of that."

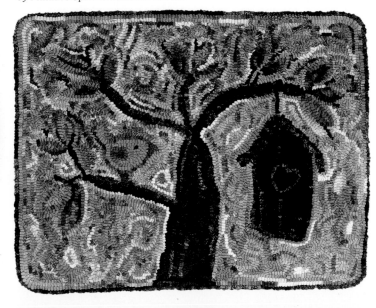

Mary and Rob's Rug. Designed and hooked by Jen Lavoie, Huntington, Vermont. 16" by 30".
"My sister-in-law has a room devoted to Korean design. At Christmas, we pick names to give gifts. She 'rigged' the pick so I would pick them, so she could get her rug!"

Back Brook Great Blue Heron. Designed and hooked by Linda Y. Sheldon, Skillman, New Jersey. 41" by 23".
"Two or three times a week, during my early morning walk along the brook behind our house, the heron who nests there steps out to make his presence known. He watches, diffident but alert, as I pass through his territory. This rug depicts him against an elegant background inspired by a Hermes china pattern."

Roosters, Hens, and Chicks

Pheasant Weathervane. Designed and hooked by Joan Hebert, Waterbury, Vermont. 24" by 15".
"The John D. Rockefeller collection has this original weathervane. I painted a reproduction and decided I had to hook one too."

Whistling Women. Designed and hooked by Dorothy Panaceck, Fredricksburg, Texas. 25" by 34".
"'Whistling women and cackling hens surely come to no good end' was a saying my mother would say to me if I whistled. I find I say it now to my granddaughter who loves to whistle."

Mali's Chicken. Designed and hooked by Joelle Hochman, Somerville, Massachusetts. 14" by 15".
"Just after my daughter Amalia was born, a friend taught me how to hook. This is my second mat, the first in a series of animal mats inspired by Amalia's great love and interest in little critters. Her nickname is Mali, and now at age two, when she sees this piece she points and yells 'chicken' in a loud, happy voice."

Left:
Les Fleurs. Designed and hooked by JoAnn Millen, Boxford, Massachusetts. 25" by 36".

Center:
Country Hens. Designed and hooked by Beverly Conway, Middlebury, Vermont. 53" by 28".

Bottom:
Speckled Hens. Hooked by Susan Gingras, Weybridge, Vermont. 49" by 24". Designed by Beverly Conway Designs. "This is a new design of Beverly's. The minute I saw it, I knew I had to hook it! I call them my newsprint chickens."

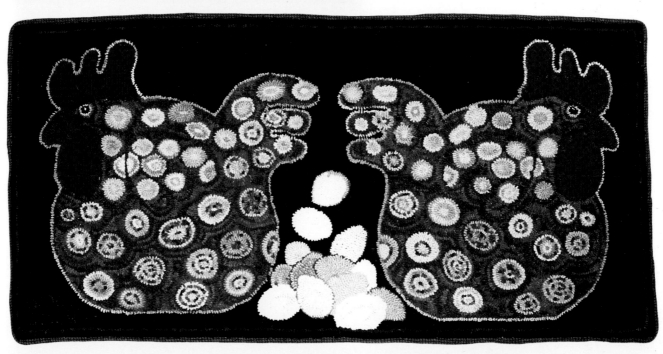

Spring Chickens. Designed and hooked by Cheryl Dulong-Wasielewski, Greenfield, Massachusetts. 30" by 16".
"Spring was my inspiration! The joy of renewal, growth, and an end to those long New England nights."

Right:
Mother's Day (No Eggs Today). Hooked by Miriam Henning, Truro, Massachusetts. 24" by 31". Designed by Patsy Becker.
"My mother had a pet chicken when she was a girl. Today she has five children and I will give her the rug for a Mother's Day gift.

Rooster Parade. Designed and hooked by Liz O'Brien of Liziana Creations, South Windsor, Connecticut. 16" by 34".

Left:
Going Against the Crowd. Designed and hooked by Polly Reinhart, Wyomissing, Pennsylvania. 33" by 27".
"The design was adapted from a quilt pattern."

Golden Chicken. Designed and hooked by Linda Repasky, Amherst, Massachusetts. 1.875" by 1.875".
"Miniature punch needle with wool thread."

B & B Roosters. Hooked by Polly Reinhart, Wyomissing, Pennsylvania. 29" by 45". Designed by Barbara Carroll.
"This rug was started in a Woolley Fox Workshop."

Hats Off to Patty. Designed and hooked by Jocelyn Guindon, Montreal, Canada. 37" by 25".
"The iconography developed by Patty Yoder inspired this rug. It is an homage to her contribution to rug hooking as an art form."

Sheep in the Meadow. Hooked by Diana M. Link, Danby, Vermont. 18" by 12". Designed by Nancy Urbanak of Beaver Brook Crafts.

Wooly Lamb. Hooked by Karen Quigley, Vergennes, Vermont. 13" by 11". Designed by Wild Goose Chase.
"This was a simple project to practice swirls and small bits of color."

Meet Miro's Friends. Designed and hooked by Davey DeGraff, Hinesburg, Vermont. 43" by 27".
"This rug was designed and made for my first precious little grandson, Miro. He is being raised a vegan and these animals will be his friends. The working title had been 'meet your meat.'"

Grazing in the Shade. Designed and hooked by Chris Gooding, South Windsor, Connecticut. 15" by 16". "I took Abby Vakay's class at Shelburne using mixed media. The sheep was a fun form to play with. She is chenille yarn and her face is clay. Her hat, the fence, and other embellishments came from the fabric store."

Rams in Flowers. Hooked by Edith McClure, Farmington, Connecticut. 36" by 26". Designed by Beverly Conway. "I started this rug in a class with Bev Conway, and with her help, changed the flowers around the rams."

Swaledale Shuffle. Hooked by Janet Santaniello, Watchung, New Jersey. 24" by 35". Designed by Sherri Heiber-Day. "I simplified the pattern by removing all except the sheep and used an uncomplicated border. Adding the lettering 'Ewe & Me,' plus the rose in the ram's mouth, added interest and pleases me. I like to think it's spring and he is courting her."

Ewe Wooly Friends. Designed and hooked by Judy Quintman, Wilmington, North Carolina. 20" by 22". "Our friendship group gets together at a rug school once a year. Last year we thought it would be fun to design something to represent our friendship. Over the few days together we came up with this design. Each of us was hooking it on their own in whatever size they wanted."

Scotland My Scotland. Hooked by Tom McNerney, Newburyport, Massachusetts. 45" by 33". Designed by Marion Ham – Quail Hill Designs.

Four Sheep. Hooked by Suzanne Pisanelli, Rutland, Vermont. 15" by 16". Designed by DiFranza Designs. "This is my first rug hooking project."

Grazing Sheep. Hooked by Deb Thomann, Gardner, Massachusetts. 16" by 10". Designed by Nancy Urbanak of Beaver Brook Crafts.

The Resourceful Knitter. Designed and hooked by Chris Gooding, South Windsor, Connecticut. 33" by 25".
"I bought this wool in Iceland where I admired the wonderful sweaters. I thought how nice it would be if an Icelandic sheep could just knit her own sweaters! This is in honor of a little friend of mine who became paralyzed in a car accident, but has become very resourceful at living a fulfilling life."

Ewe Too. Hooked by Diane S. Learmonth, Newton, Iowa. 26" by 21". Designed by Faith Williston for Primco Patterns.
"Ewe Too was hooked using 'as is' wool – much of it is vintage and quite thick. The free shape called to me."

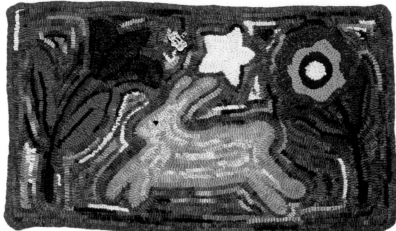

Bunny in the Spring. Hooked by Karen Quigley, Vergennes, Vermont. 24" by 14". Designed by Breezy Ridge Rugs. "Bunny in the spring garden – my love of animals and gardening combined with bright colors of spring."

Mister Hare. Hooked by Tricia Tague Miller, Alstead, New Hampshire. 25" by 25". Barbara Carroll's Warren Kimble pattern. "Warren Kimble's work has a certain whimsy that appeals to me. Just look at the expression on this hare's face! This was a fun, relaxing project executed completely from odds and ends of wools. The background was a tartan skirt from the Salvation Army that I overdyed."

Morris Rabbit Pillow. Hooked by Ruth Frost, East Montpelier, Vermont. 12" by 16". Designed by Jane McGown Flynn.

Billy Bunny's Fortune. Hooked by Debra Kaiser, Shelburne, Vermont. 45" by 25". Design interpreted by Debra Kaiser from an illustration by Maginel Wright Enright. "I have always loved the illustrations of Maginel Wright Enright, a successful artist, designer, and needleworker born in 1877. Her composition, color, and playful and fanciful subject matter is a delight to see. My interpretation is based on an illustration from the children's book, *Billy Bunny's Fortune*, published in 1919.

Tortoise and the Hare. Designed and hooked by Mary Jameson, Brattleboro, Vermont. 13" diameter. "Traced rabbit, drew turtle. First try at hooking."

Bunny Love. Hooked by Karen Quigley, Vergennes, Vermont. 16" by 14". Designed by Karen Kahle and Primitive Spirit.
"Primitive Spirit's version of a bunny in the garden appealed to my love of animals and the primitive look of hooking."

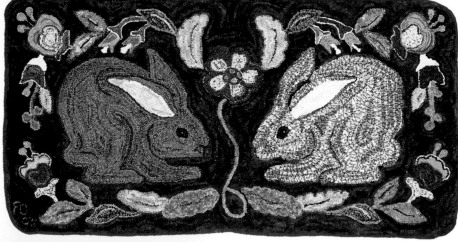

Bunnies Two. Hooked by Fran Oken, Middletown Springs, Vermont. 45" by 24". Designed by Patsy Becker.

Nora's Bunny. Designed and hooked by Celia Y. Oliver, Shelburne, Vermont. 22" by 30".
"My daughter, Nora, now age sixteen, adopted her first bunny when she was two weeks old. Now that she has collected bunnies of every size, shape, color and material, it seemed only right that I should hook a rabbit for the family. The pattern is based on a nineteenth century Staffordshire ceramic rabbit."

115

Once In a Blue Moon. Hooked by Susan Charbonneau, Kinderhook, New York. 36" by 25". Designed by Jan Gassner and adapted by Susan Charbonneau.
"I love fantasy! The Hare is soaring over my house and over a scene of the Catskill Mountains."

Horses ———————

Red Rocking Horse. Hooked by Kristina Burnett, Canaan, New Hampshire. 36" by 46". Designer unknown.
"Adapted from a c.1885 hooked rug shown in *American Hooked and Sewn Rugs: Folk Art Underfoot,* by Joel and Kate Kopp."

Below:
Spirit Ponies. Designed and hooked by Gail Majauckas, West Newbury, Massachusetts. 27" by 17".
"Inspired by colors and motifs in the Southwest."

116

Rocky II the Rocking Horse. Designed and hooked by Deb Thomann, Gardner, Massachusetts. 12" by 13".
"I purchased a youth chair to match my kitchen for my first grandchild. I decided to make a chair pad for the chair. I hope this will turn into a family heirloom! I enjoyed making this special gift for my special boy."

Pegasus. Designed and hooked by Pat Merikallio, New Canaan, Connecticut. 43" by 39".
"My granddaughter wanted me to do a rug with Pegasus so I obliged. I added Medusa because she was Pegasus' mother. The scene at the bottom is of Greece as I remember it with a monastery and a temple."

Horse in the Garden. Hooked by Deb Kelley, Shoreham, Vermont. 18" by 12". Designed by Nancy Urbanak.

George's Horse. Designed and hooked by Judith B. Bush, Woodstock, Vermont. 46" by 34".
"My former neighbor, George, had a wooden cutout of this horse attached to his workshop door."

117

Horse with No Name. Designed and hooked by Lucille B. Festa, Wilton, Connecticut. 48" by 23".
"A song from the 1970s and an old weathervane were my inspiration."

Donkeys in 'Natural' Garden. Designed and hooked by Evelyn Lawrence, Hallstead, Pennsylvania. 53" by 27".
"I snapped a photo of these donkeys while driving in the countryside."

Chapter 6

Geometrics

Log Cabin (Red Series #2). Karen Baxter Cooper, New London, New Hampshire. 40" by 18". Design adapted by Karen Baxter Cooper from an antique rug, c.1920.

"My love of quilting and an old rug in *American Hooked and Sewn Rugs: Folk Art Underfoot,* by Joel and Kate Kopp inspired this rug."

Chrysanthemum (Red Series #3). Hooked by Karen Baxter Cooper, New London, New Hampshire. 40" by 17". Design adapted by Karen Baxter Cooper from an antique rug, c.1880.

"This is one of the three rugs hooked to cover the window seats in my working room in North Carolina. The design, from *American Hooked and Sewn Rugs: Folk Art Underfoot,* by Joel and Kate Kopp worked well for this shape."

My Stars! Hooked by Karen Baxter Cooper, New London, New Hampshire. 42" by 18". Design adapted by Karen Baxter Cooper from an antique rug, c.1885.

"A nineteenth century rug in *American Hooked and Sewn Rugs: Folk Art Underfoot,* by Joel and Kate Kopp inspired this rug – one of the three hooked to cover my window seats. The background pattern of hit or miss stars is my original idea."

French Bowties. Designed and hooked by Diana M. Link, Danby, Vermont. 37" by 14".
"This design was the result of a class taken from Gail Dufresne on geometrics."

Log Cabin. Hooked by Evelyn Lawrence, Hallstead, Pennsylvania. 48" by 48". Design adapted by Evelyn Lawrence.
"Geometric pattern based on an old quilting design called 'Log Cabin'."

Leftover Purples. Hooked by Suzi Prather, Orlando, Florida. 43" by 36". Design adapted by Suzi Prather from a traditional quilt pattern.
"I started this rug in a class with Gail Dufresne as my teacher. I was just trying to use a lot of my beautiful purple wools."

Nine Block Rug. Designed and hooked by Nancy Ellingham, Batavia, New York. 44" by 25".
"I like to do geometric designs and this was a good way to use up all my leftover cut wool. The color combination (warm and cool) was fun to do."

Josephine's Garden. Designed and hooked by Laurilyn Wiles – Vermont Folk Rugs, Hinesburg, Vermont. 45" by 32".
"Josephine's Garden was designed for a special little girl, Josephine Rose. It is my hope that this rug will bring her happy thoughts and be an enduring reminder of a grandmother's love."

Tumbling Blocks #3. Designed and hooked by Marilyn Bottjer, Eastchester, New York. 42" by 31".
"Inspired by quilt designs."

Bright Lights. Designed and hooked by Sue Hammond, New London, New Hampshire. 37" by 24".
"This is an adaptation of a quilt design. I named it for the light bright colors of the small squares. It was made as a demonstration project while artisan-in-residence at Enfield Shaker Museum, Enfield, New Hampshire."

Antique Stars. Hooked by Alan S. Kidder, Rochester, Vermont. 57" by 34". Designer unknown.
"My aunt, Eula Harvey, gave me this rug pattern in 1973. It was purchased from Anne Ashworth's shop. I love geometrics, but the size and repetitive pattern took its toll as it took me thirty years to complete. It was my first rug – started in 1973 and finished in 2003."

Utopian Dream. Designed and hooked by Lori Lupe Pelish, Niskayuna, New York. 72" by 65".
"Imagine standing on the brink of a primordial garden with the earth and man's capacity ready to unfold."

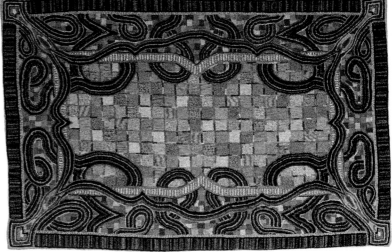

Radiant Reflection. Designed and hooked by Lori Lupe Pelish, Niskayuna, New York. 69" by 45".
"An inspiring fall day with a peerless blue sky reflecting off the lichen covered trees."

Royal Promenade. Designed and hooked by Lori Lupe Pelish, Niskayuna, New York. 72" by 50".
"My thoughts revolved around creating a balance from opposites. The mixture of organic forms with geometric shapes are further enhanced by the complementary reds and greens."

Graphic Floral #1. Designed and hooked by Susan Lampe-Wilson, Trumbull, Connecticut. 20" by 20".
"Created as a 'hit or miss' piece to use only materials I had on hand. I used a #9 punch to outline and a #10 to fill so the outlines show up better. I was inspired by a penny rug I saw in *American Folk Art* by W. Ketchum, Jr. for the flower with heart shaped leaves."

Seven Stars. Designed and hooked by Devin Ryder, Somerville, Massachusetts. 35" by 29".
"This is an abstract representation of the seven chakras or 'interior stars' within the physical body. They are: Mercury (pineal gland), yellow; Moon (pituitary), blue; Venus (throat), green; Sun (heart), orange; Jupiter (solar plexus), violet; Mars (pelvis), red; and Saturn (base of spine), indigo. The triangles represent mountains, which symbolize our journey towards spiritual goals."

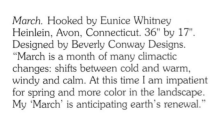

March. Hooked by Eunice Whitney Heinlein, Avon, Connecticut. 36" by 17". Designed by Beverly Conway Designs. "March is a month of many climactic changes: shifts between cold and warm, windy and calm. At this time I am impatient for spring and more color in the landscape. My 'March' is anticipating earth's renewal."

123

Geometric Bicycle Wheels. Designed and hooked by Deb Kelley, Shoreham, Vermont. 8" by 8".

Parcheesi Board. Hooked by Deb Kelley, Shoreham, Vermont. 24" by 36". Designed by Beverly Conway Designs.

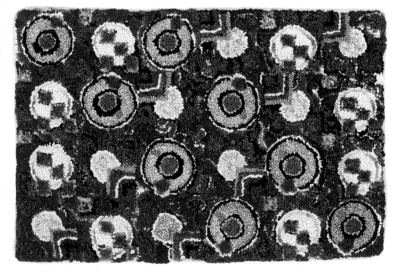

Linoleum. Designed and hooked by Anne-Marie Littenberg, Burlington, Vermont. 20" by 29".
"This was a study in combining yarn and wool, using the Oxford Punch Needle. I also wanted to explore my hatred of green and purple. I now adore these colors. The pattern reminds me of old linoleum I found in my 1927 house."

Checkerboard. Hooked by Rebecca Erb, Sinking Spring, Pennsylvania. 60" by 27".
Designed by Evelyn Lawrence for Beverly Conway Designs.
"This rug was started at a Wooley Fox Retreat with help from Barb Carroll."

Geo Mat II. Designed and hooked by Sarah J. McNamara, Greenport, New York. 8" by 8".
"I designed this mat as part of a swap on 'Padula,' the Internet bulletin board for rug hookers. I enjoyed hooking and sculpting it so much, I made another to keep for myself!"

Primitive Geometric. Hooked by Cyndi Melendy Labelle, Hinesburg, Vermont. 24" by 24". Designed by Vermont Folk Rugs.

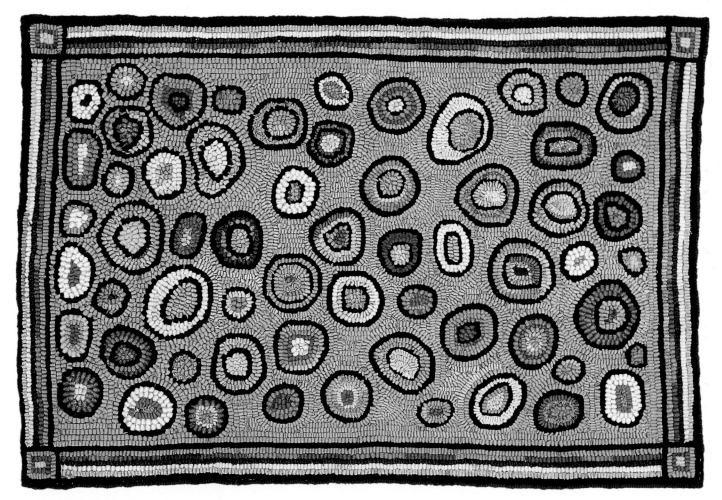

Summer Days. Designed and hooked by Miriam Henning, Truro, Massachusetts. 35" by 24".
"I hooked this rug during July and August. There are a little over sixty circles – each represents a summer vacation day, each is different and beautiful, no two just alike. My first rug."

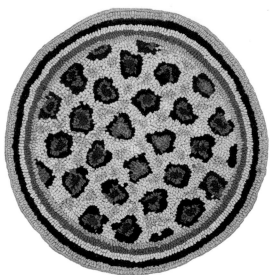

Left:
Abstract Chair Pad. Hooked by Jane B. Clarke, Brattleboro, Vermont. 15" diameter. Designer unknown.
"This was my first attempt at rug hooking. It was an easy design for a new hooker."

Center:
Scrap Circles. Designed and hooked by Kathleen Patten, Hinesburg, Vermont. 54" by 28".
"I did this rug to force myself to use blues. I tend to avoid them for no known reason."

Bottom:
Basket Weave Mat. Designed and hooked by Gail Duclos Lapierre, Shelburne, Vermont. 17" by 42".
"This rug is the prototype for my 'Basket Weave Runner'. I wasn't sure if the design would give the basket weave effect I was wanting and I had never tried the 3/8" cut. I used the same eight wools in the same order in each rectangle."

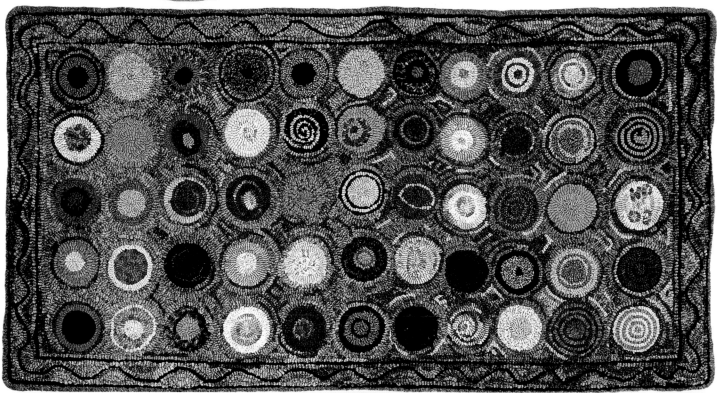

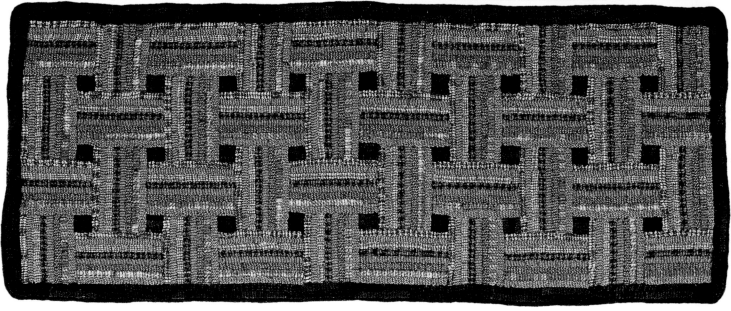

Basket Weave Runner. Designed and hooked by Gail Duclos Lapierre, Shelburne, Vermont. 127" by 34".

"I amass a lot of gray when recycling wool. I needed a runner for my hall, which just happens to be gray! Being a frugal Vermonter, I didn't want to waste backing – I hooked across the width. When I was close to the selvedge I overlapped the next piece and hooked through both layers to continue on."

Random Basket Weave. Designed and hooked by Maureen Yates, South Burlington, Vermont. 30" by 24".

"My original inspiration was a huge bag of strips cut for other rugs. Final modifications were inspired by the 'Hinesburg Hookers,' who never fail to encourage each other and anyone who is lucky enough to show up on a Monday night."

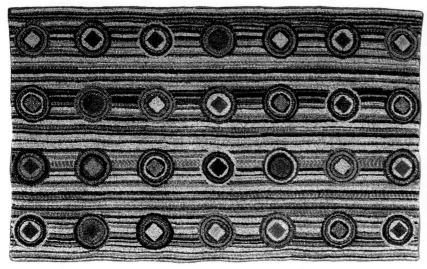

Geometric. Hooked by Evelyn S. Lawrence, Hallstead, Pennsylvania. 60" by 37". Adapted from an antique geometric design.

Ethiopian Angels. Designed and hooked by Preston McAdoo of McAdoo Rugs, North Bennington, Vermont. 92" by 32".
"Inspired by African art."

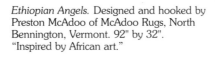

127

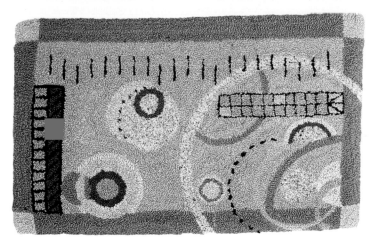

Frank's Geometry. Designed and hooked by Anne-Marie Littenberg, Burlington, Vermont. 22" by 35".
"This is the rug I hooked while learning to use the Oxford Punch Needle. I was inspired by my love for the textiles and glass designed by Frank Lloyd Wright."

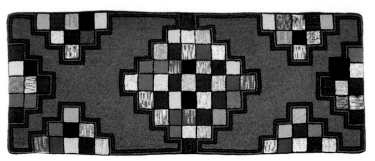

Remembering Grandma. Hooked by Alan S. Kidder, Rochester, Vermont. 54" by 21". Designed by Julia Kidder.
"My grandmother, Julia Kidder, hooked this geometric rug in 1928 on burlap. I copied her pattern and color scheme and hooked a replica in 2003 on linen. Size, pattern, design, and color remain the same. Grandma lives on."

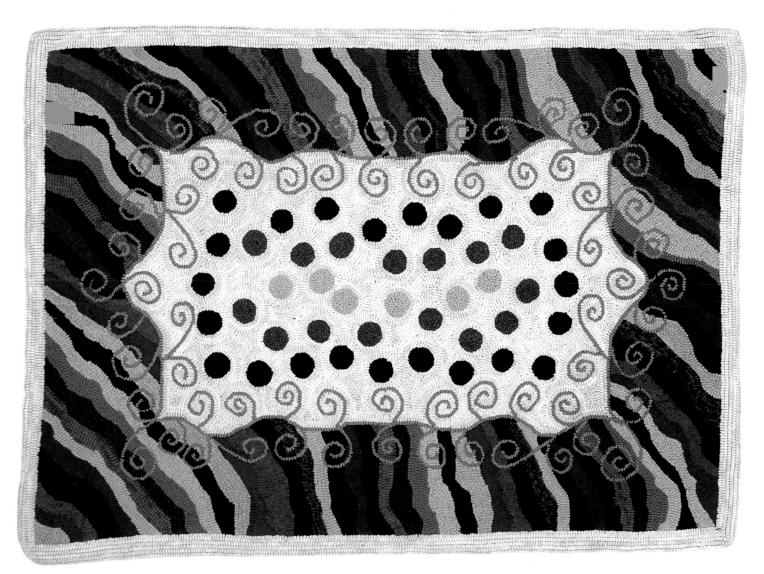

Autumn Waves. Hooked by Bev Lary, Rochester, Vermont. 30" by 45". Adapted by Bev Lary from a picture in *Home Decorators.*
"The colors caught my eye. I freehanded the design and with thrift shop wool and fill-in colors from Bev Conway, I combined fall colors to frame a soft center. It reminds me of pebbles in water that ripple to the shore and explore into fall leaves."

128

Kazak-Istan. Hooked by Tony Latham, Montreal, Quebec, Canada. 35" by 16". Designed by Jane McGown Flynn.

Memories of Buzz. Designed and hooked by Priscilla Buzzell, Newport, Vermont. 33" by 13". "My husband, Hall Buzzell, passed away December 29, 2002. I decided to make each of my children a small rug using his garments in a basket weave pattern, which I did and gave to them for Christmas in 2003. Then I wanted something for myself so I designed an inch rug with the materials, mostly a favorite orange hunting coat. The grids and outside border are his uniform pants from many years of teaching at Norwich University."

Aztec Aviary. Designed and hooked by Jocelyn Guindon, Montreal, Quebec, Canada. 47" by 30".
"Pre-Columbian iconography inspired this rug. I also wanted to experiment with textures for the background (basket weave, herringbone, diagonals, etc.)."

Tibetan Amdo-Caravan Rug. Designed and hooked by Jocelyn Guindon, Montreal, Quebec, Canada. 62" by 45".
"Inspired by a traditional saddle rug from Tibet."

Omar Khayyam. Hooked by Helen Wolfel, Barre, Vermont. Designed by Pearl McGown.
"I found this pattern in Moshimer's bargain box in February, 2003. I decided to hook it for my daughter, Lurlene, for her home. I used lots of 'as is,' plaids and very little dyed wool. Orientals are fun to work on, outline, and fill."

Bessarabian. Hooked by Molly W. Dye, Jacksonville, Vermont. 43" by 29". Designed by Jane McGown Flynn.

Afshar. Hooked by Karen L. Maddi-Perks, Chicago, Illinois. 50" by 36". Designed by Ruth R. Hall.
"I love the shapes of oriental style rugs but I prefer rich colors. I enjoyed trying to include as many colors as I could in this rug and was fascinated by the complexity that emerged as I added more colors. I incorporate rich, highly saturated colors in all my rugs."

Antique Weathervanes. Designed and hooked by Gwen Kjelleren, South Hero, Vermont. 44" by 44".
"I was inspired to dye some of my wool 'stash' by the wonderful colors in the Vermont Folk Rug's book, *Dyeing to Get Primitive Colors on Wool.* The design for the rug was inspired by the simple folk art quality of antique weathervanes."

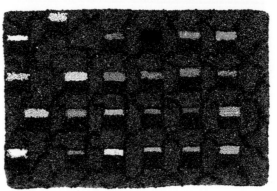

Home Depot Sampler.
Designed and hooked by
Anne-Marie Littenberg,
Burlington, Vermont. 29" by
20".
"This rug resulted from a
shopping spree at Home
Depot where I picked up a
variety of materials I thought
were 'cool' and incorporated
them: copper and brass wire,
hemp, plastic, mylar, nylon
cord, etc."

Ming. Hooked by Baily Ruckert, Wellfleet, Massachusetts.
56" by 34". Designed by Pearl McGown.
"I enjoyed having an ongoing oriental to hook. My
beloved teacher, Gloria Hautanen, color planned 'Ming'
for me and it is my final rug under her tutelage."

Em's Oriental. Hooked by Joan Wheeler, Newport, Vermont. 19" by 43". Designed by Green
Mountain Rugs.
"Oriental done for my granddaughter after seeing this rug done in Helen Wolfel's class."

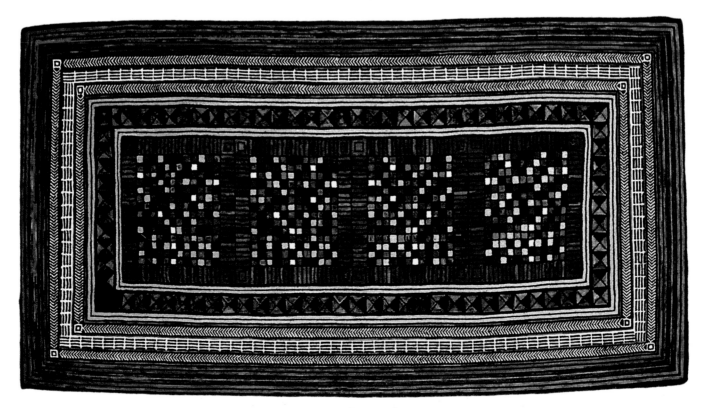

Egypt 1. Designed and hooked by Elizabeth Guth, Tunbridge, Vermont. 60" by 30".
"Geometric motifs from Egyptian tomb walls."

Chapter 7

Pictorials

Cedar in Hayfield. Designed and hooked by Anne-Marie Littenberg, Burlington, Vermont. 20" by 28".
"This is the first rug where I dyed or over-dyed all the wool myself. I am working on a series of rugs that incorporate different trees. Some of my traditional hooker friends thought I had pulled the loops. They were mistaken. This was made with a number six cut wool and The Oxford Punch Needle."

Poplar. Designed and hooked by
Anne-Marie Littenberg,
Burlington, Vermont. 9" by 9".

Beyond the Garden Gate. Designed and hooked by Anne-Marie Littenberg, Burlington, Vermont. 22" by 26".
"Vermont gardens are spectacular and so are the views beyond them. The sugar maple was inspired by one on the grounds of Shelburne Museum. This was punch-hooked using dozens of threads per loop, and dozens and dozens of stitches or loops per square inch."

Lane's Island. Designed and hooked by Carol Morris Petillo, Vinalhaven, Maine. 30" by 32".
"I live on an island in the Penobscot Bay with many beautiful vistas. One of the loveliest is a nature preserve on a connected island where we walk our dogs and enjoy views across the bay to Matincus. This rug is a loosely imagined, impressionist-inspired, version of this view."

Autumn on Middle Mountain. Designed and hooked by Carol Morris Petillo, Vinalhaven, Maine. 40" by 24".
"I live on an island in the Penobscot Bay with many beautiful vistas. We often walk our dogs in Middle Mountain Park, one of the highest points on the island where, in the fall, the huckleberry bushes turn blazing oranges and reds. This rug was inspired by the view from Middle Mountain across Penobscot Bay to the Camden Hills."

Sunset Tree. Designed and hooked by Beverly J. Delnicki, Wheelock, Vermont. 13" by 18".
"I love trees and have done them in needlepoint and crewel. This is my hooked tree."

Yonder Mountain. Hooked by Deb Kelley, Shoreham, Vermont. 24" by 48". Design adapted by Deb Kelley from the book *Yonder Mountain*, written by Kay Thorpe Bannon and illustrated by Kristina Rodanas.

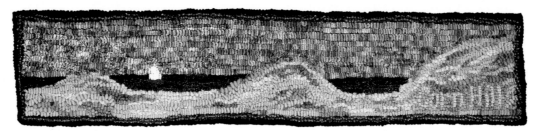

Corn Hill Dunes. Designed and hooked by Miriam Henning, Truro, Massachusetts. 5" by 24".
"My view while at work."

Carol's Rug. Designed and hooked by Jen Lavoie, Huntington, Vermont. 24" by 10".
"My mother-in-law lives in Florida during the winter and often leaves before peak color – so I hooked a little bit of Vermont for her."

Sketch - Winter Scene. Designed and hooked by Jen Lavoie, Huntington, Vermont. 11" by 8".

135

Sailor's Homecoming. Hooked by Amy Spokes, South Burlington, Vermont. 60" diameter. Designed by Joan Moshimer.

Below:
The Flying Cloud. Hooked by Claire Walker, Proctorsville, Vermont. 45" by 34". Designed by Harry M. Fraser Company.
"I started this project in 1963 at Harry Fraser Studios in Manchester, Connecticut. Two years later, we were transferred out of state, and I lost my network. This project went in my attic for thirty-eight years, finally landing in Proctorsville where we retired. My dream to finish it came alive two years ago when I met Amy Oxford at Fletcher Farm School for the Arts and Crafts. With her inspiration, I worked to finish it forty years later!"

Left:
Cape Cod Oriental. Designed and hooked by Shirley Wiedemann, East Falmouth, Massachusetts. 31" by 23".
"This design was inspired by my imagination."

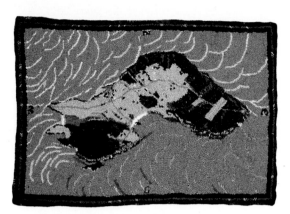

East Ironbound Island. Designed and hooked by Susan Alain, Montreal, Quebec, Canada. 27" by 38".
"Aerial photograph – I have a house on this island. My first rug."

Yankee Clipper. Hooked by Denise W. Jose, Keuka Park, New York. 26" by 35". Barbara Carroll's Warren Kimble pattern.
"My husband chose this rug and requested that I have a sunset for a background. He had lots of input along the way, including the addition of the rope border."

137

The Morgan Rally Challenge. Designed and hooked by Lelia F. Ridgway, Downington, Pennsylvania. 54" by 38".

"This is a story rug about the time I was the rally master for the Morgan sports car club rally on a beautiful October day. A Morgan is an English sports car. In a rally, one is given a set of confusing instructions to complete the course and end up at a specific location at a predetermined time. It sounds very simple, but you would be amazed at what can happen, as evidenced in the rug."

A Week at Camp. Hooked by Susan Charbonneau, Kinderhook, New York. 36" by 28". Designed by Patsy Becker.

138

Cow and Lupine. Hooked by Pam Bartlett, Loudon, New Hampshire. 30" by 28". Designed by Deanne Fitzpatrick.

Nova Scotia Coast. Hooked by Eunice Whitney Heinlein, Avon, Connecticut. 37" by 29". Design adapted by Highland Heart Hookery.

"Maude Lewis was a folk artist in Nova Scotia. Her designs are owned by the Art Gallery of Nova Scotia which has licensed Highland Heart Hookery to use them for rug designs."

Ladies' Tea. Hooked by Arlene Scanlon, Essex Junction, Vermont. 29" by 32". Designed by Patsy Becker.

Winnie's Home. Designed and hooked by Sue Janssen, Benson, Vermont. 19" by 17".

"In October 2003, I visited my friends Janice and Reg Puckett at their home in Warren Connecticut. I took a picture from their front porch and it became the basis for this pillow, which will be their 2004 Christmas present. The reason for my visit that weekend was to meet their new puppy, Winnie."

Seasons. Designed and hooked by Bev Lary, Rochester, Vermont. 25" by 35".

"I love the seasons of Vermont. I designed a picture as seen through a window. The four panes have the same tree showing the four seasons."

Chaco Canyon. Designed and hooked by Baily Ruckert, Wellfleet, Massachusetts. 37" by 27".

"In traveling through New Mexico, I came upon the ancient ruins of the Chaco Indians. I was not only fascinated with the patterns in the stones, but also with the play of light through the doorways and windows. Ann Winterling dyed the wool and helped with the design, and Jan Seavey designed the border."

Dreams. Designed and hooked by Bev Lary, Rochester, Vermont. 18" by 25".

"I love the winter moons and needed a small picture to hang above my bed."

The Cars of Our Life. Designed and hooked by Sarah Province, Silver Spring, Maryland. 38" by 28".
"This rug is for our grandson, Phil, who is named for my husband. The design began with my husband's 1938 Plymouth Coupe, his prized possession. He rode in it as a young child, learned to drive in it, and it was his only car until the 1960s. Jule Marie Smith helped develop the border of cars that were important in our life. The house is Phil's home in West Virginia and the flowers were tended by his mother. My daughter (little Phil's mother) used our Chrysler New Yorker (lower left) for her wedding and the green truck (lower right) shows the baby coming home from the hospital."

Olde English. Hooked by Gail Papetti, Newport Center, Vermont. 27" by 37". Designed by Green Mountain Rugs.

Ruth's Kitchen. Hooked by Mary Parker, Yorktown Heights, New York. 28" by 33". Designed by Mary Parker (with templates designed by Deanne Fitzpatrick used in the border).

"This rug is a memory of my grandmother's farmhouse in Wisconsin. As children, we liked to help her in the kitchen. We could see the farm buildings out the window. My grandfather always drove a Cadillac. The border reflects my grandmother's great love for her garden."

Glendale, Ohio. Designed and hooked by Alberta Strauss, Waitsfield, Vermont. 96" by 48".

Alberta Strauss learned to hook in the early 1980s, choosing as her first project scenes from her hometown of Glendale, Ohio. A lifelong artist, Alberta had no difficulty sketching the most important buildings in her beloved hometown. Alberta says, "Glendale Ohio is one of the first planned communities in the country. Men drove by horse and buggy to the railroad station to catch the train to go to work in Cincinnati. Little children were allowed to watch the trains and greet their fathers on their return. The trains and the children's clothes are typical of the nineteenth century. Though a tiny village, Glendale has seven active churches. All are depicted in the rug." Alberta took several years researching, sketching, and dyeing the wool for the rug. Unfortunately, the project slowed as the burlap on which she hooked began to split. The project stopped altogether when she left her home in Ohio for an assisted living situation nearer her son in Vermont. In 2003, Alberta and her son attended the rug hooking show at Shelburne Museum and met Stephanie Krauss of Montpelier, Vermont, who agreed to repair the splits, finish the hooking, and give the rug a new backing of linen.

Cloverdale Plantation. Hooked by Nola A. Heidbreder, Saint Louis, Missouri. 54" by 36". Designed by Linda Pietz of Cactus Needle.
"I wanted to make a large rug using just 'as is' Pendleton shirts and skirts."

Ashuelot Bridge. Designed and hooked by Sheila M. Breton, Surry, New Hampshire. 27" by 20".
"Ashuelot is a bridge I used to walk across to school. The school is at the end of the bridge. I hooked it as it used to be prior to a renovation. The frame (not shown here) was made by my husband, Frederick Breton."

Lake Compounce. Designed and hooked by Nancy Norton, Avon, Connecticut. 64" by 40".
"Lake Compounce, a family amusement park located in Bristol, Connecticut, was founded by the Norton Family in 1846. Still operating today, though not by the Nortons, it is the oldest continuously operating amusement park in the United States. The merry-go-round is on the National Historic Register. I have tried to recreate it as it is remembered by my family in the 1940s and 1950s."

Books At Our House. Designed and hooked by Joanne Miller, Canaan, New Hampshire. 96" by 30".
"For the longest time, I've wanted to hook a pictorial rug of the historic buildings on my street. As a trial run, I hooked them as bookends in a bookcase pattern that I drew for a runner in the hallway to our den. The top of the rug is our 1803 house, below that is the Canaan Museum, followed by bookends of the Canaan Meeting House and the Old North Church. Chloe, our lab, awaits you."

Well Heeled Ladies. Designed and hooked by Burma Cassidy, Rochester, Vermont. 14" by 13".
"These are the shoes of the rich and famous: Marilyn Monroe (being stalked by a shadow), Judy Garland (who finally went over the rainbow), Madonna, and *Sex and the City* queen Sara Jessica Parker."

Sacred Kingdom. Designed and hooked by Susan Longchamps, West Burke, Vermont. 24" by 17".
"After many years of interest and admiration for Native American Indians, I decided to design and hook a rug showing the culmination of the Indian cultures."

Right:
Chinese Jar. Designed and hooked by Shirley Chaiken, Lebanon, New Hampshire. 28" by 22".
"I got the inspiration for the flowered jar from the knitting graph in a book of home decor ideas."

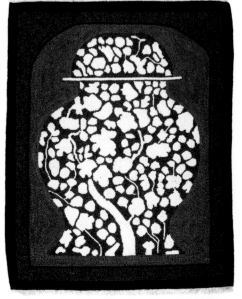

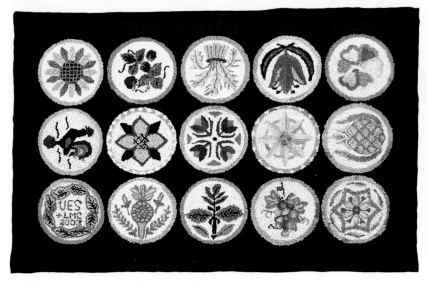

Buttermolds. Hooked by Victoria E. Simpson, Bath, Maine. 40" by 26". Designed by Joan Moshimer.

"This is an old Joan Moshimer pattern. She also did a buttermold pattern that was nearly twice as big. The colors are all of my own choosing. It is my first rug."

Doodle Rug. Hooked by Jean MacQuiddy, Weston, Massachusetts. 24" by 36". Designed by Noriko Manago.

"In the 2003 Shelburne workshop with Rae Harrell, Noriko created the doodle design. As a gift she made one for me too. I did the color planning and hooking. Helen Jeffrey did the braided edge."

Josiah Turner Cobbler Sign. Hooked by Dick LaBarge, Victory Mills, New York. 52" by 22". Design adapted by George Kahnle for Hooked on the Creek.

"This rug is an adaptation of a sign in the Abby Aldrich Rockefeller Museum at Williamsburg, Virginia. Used as a cobbler's sign, it is typical of the 19th century signs that are so valuable and collectible by today's folk art collectors."

Abbie's Alphabet. Hooked by Margery Kimpton, Dunstable, Massachusetts. 74" by 36". Designed by Abbie Clark and Margery Kimpton.

"Perhaps one of the most magical years of life is spent in first grade. Certainly it was so for Abbie. The drawings she brought home every day were, if not quite Picassos or Monets, proof of her whimsical imagination and inexhaustible charm. Grandma suggested that Abbie make a drawing for each letter of the alphabet – they were transformed into this rug, using Abbie's best first grade printing."

"One morning, Abbie and Grandma took the rug to first grade, with other examples of rug hooking, rug warp, wool strips, and hooks, so that everyone could try rug hooking. But the best fun was when all the boys and girls 'jumped out' their names, a game Abbie had invented: spelling out her name and other words by jumping sequentially on the appropriate letters in the rug ... a rug hooker's own version of hopscotch!"

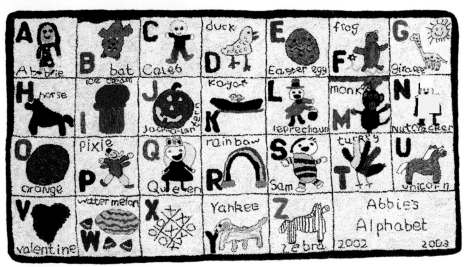

Excess on Occasion Is Exhilarating. Designed and hooked by Diane Kelly, Dorset, Vermont. 60" by 18".
"This rug is a result of a class on 'Humor in Rugs' with Emily Robertson, followed by a class on punch hooking with Amy Oxford. 'Excess on Occasion is Exhilarating' is my wool stash motto as these shelves full of color and texture indicate. The center is punch hooked working from the back. The use of unusual yarns created the explosive effect around the words."

Jack. Designed and hooked by Donna Andrews-Maness, Falmouth, Massachusetts. 26" by 26".
"This is a first attempt at hooking and is inspired by my son, who started life in Korea with the name Jung, Joo Hyuk, and is now and will forever be known as Jack. Patchwork quilting and the four points of the compass are design influences."

Center of Light Star. Designed and hooked by Claire O'Classen, Center of Light, Wallingford, Vermont. 30" by 37".
"The seven pointed star was given to The Center as its divine symbol for higher learning."

Totem. Designed and hooked by Lynn Ocone, Burlington, Vermont. 36" by 26".
"This rug is adapted from a 1700s Pennsylvania German or Pennsylvania Dutch motif, combined with symbols of personal significance."

146

Right:

The Cloths of Heaven. Designed and hooked by Penny Cunningham, South Hero, Vermont. 37" diameter.

"My inspiration was the poem 'Aedh Wishes for the Cloths of Heaven' by W.B. Yeats:

> Had I the heavens' embroidered cloths,
> Enwrought with golden and silver light,
> The blue and the dim and the dark cloths
> Of night and light and the half light,
> I would spread the cloths under your feet:
> But I, being poor, have only my dreams;
> I have spread my dreams under your feet;
> Tread softly because you tread on my dreams.

Below:

The Nine. Designed and hooked by Barbara Held, Tinmouth, Vermont. 38" by 44".

"This piece fulfills two intentions: to hook a piece for the wall behind my husband's telescope, and to hook something indicative of the nine members in my hooking group. I wanted sparkle in my universe and used many different fabrics that would reflect light."

147

Graduation. Hooked by Barbara Ludwig, Belmont, Vermont. 31" by 24". Designed by Linda Potvin and Barbara Ludwig. "I hooked this rug for our daughter, Jamie, who will be graduating from Colorado College in May. I want her to know how much we love her and how proud we are of all her accomplishments, which I try to show through this rug."

Noah's Ark. Hooked by Judith English, Cornwall, Vermont. 18" by 22". Designed by Barbara Carroll. Original art by Carol Endres.

Blue Willow. Hooked by Jane Clarke, Brattleboro, Vermont. Designed by Joan Moshimer. 14" diameter. "I have collected Blue Willow and blue dishes so this chair seat design was perfect. Thank you Joan Moshimer for this pattern."

Pear. Designed and hooked by Burma Cassidy, Rochester, Vermont. 21" by 17". "I designed this pear and border – I love the colors."

Left Behind by Noah and the Ark. Hooked by Elizabeth Morgan, Wallingford, Vermont. 28" by 22". Designed by Elizabeth Morgan, Claire O'Classen, and Diane Aines. "I was challenged to do a Noah's Ark rug and got my inspiration from a song written by The Irish Rovers."

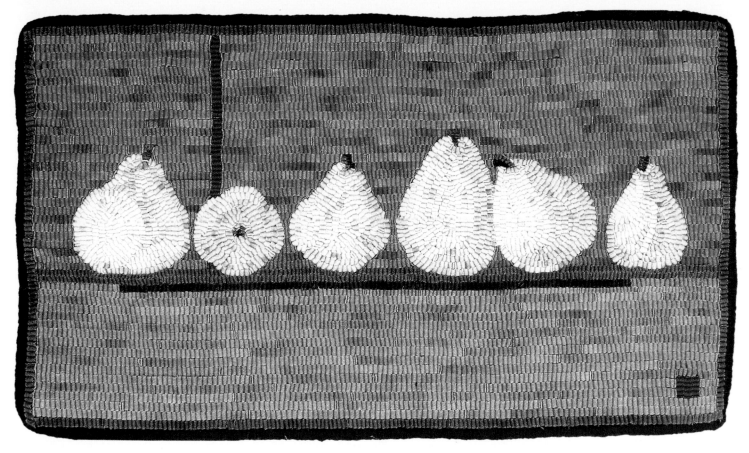

Wooden Pears. Designed and hooked by Polly S. Alexander, Essex Junction, Vermont. 23" by 13".
"I've always been attracted to Asian Minimalism, Mondrian, and the Shakers' sense of simplicity. When I came upon a set of wooden pears, I admired their pure form. I dream of a future free of clutter with just a few simple rugs and of course, piles and piles of wool!"

Oh Pear. Designed and hooked by Burma Cassidy, Rochester, Vermont. 17" by 17".
"This piece combines punch needle and flannel wool hooking. I love the round feminine shapes of pears."

Work from the Hand. Designed and hooked by Barbara Held, Tinmouth, Vermont. 10" by 26".
"This piece was a present for my son, who's a dentist. I wanted something to go over his front door and to match the colors in his living room. Cookie cutters were my inspiration. I basically used leftover wool."

Where the Heart Is. Designed and hooked by Barbara Held, Tinmouth, Vermont. 10" by 26".
"This piece was a present for my older son who was expecting his first child. He is very 'home oriented' and this hanging was made for his living room. I used wool that was left over from other work. Cookie cutters again inspired me."

149

Some members of the Green Mountain Rug Hooking Guild on the opening night of the rug show. The back drop is Anne-Marie Littenberg's "Farm Garden With Distant Passing Storm." Fortunately, no storms, distant or otherwise, spoiled our gala – it was a beautiful Vermont spring evening.

The Gleaner. Designed and hooked by Burma Cassidy, Rochester, Vermont. 21" by 24".

"The gleaner lives in a world of reinvention. She gathers up that which people no longer love and infuses new life and hope into them."

150

The Immigrant. Designed and hooked by Burma Cassidy, Rochester, Vermont. 29" by 21".
"The immigrant is all of our ancestors leaving behind the familiar and moving into the great unknown, filled with hope and longing for a better life."

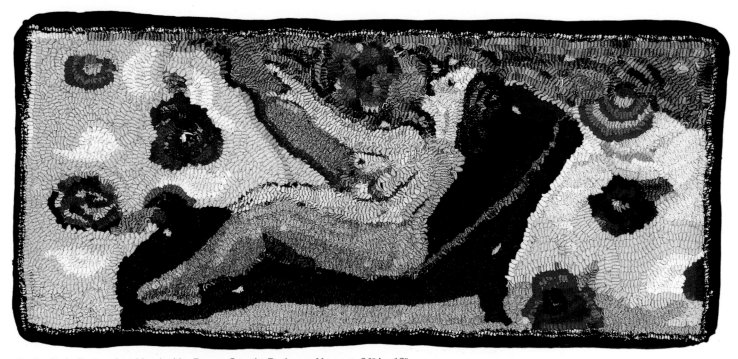

Garden Bath. Designed and hooked by Burma Cassidy, Rochester, Vermont. 26" by 12".
"Garden bath is a fantasy: bathing, sunning, air filled with floral fragrance, young green leaves drifting in the gentle breeze falling into spring green grass."

Cherished Child. Designed and hooked by Eugenie Delaney, North Ferrisburg, Vermont. 44" by 30".

"My daughter, Maddie, has been a joy since the day she came into this world. The words 'I love you' slip easily from her lips for her family, two and four legged. I hooked this rug to honor her beautiful spirit. I am truly blessed to be the mother of this cherished child."

Wildflower (top) and *Moving On* (bottom). Designed and hooked by Sharon L. Townsend, Altoona, Iowa. 50" by 29" and 25" by 29" respectively.

"This rug (top) evolved from a face peeking through the flowers into a lady walking in a garden up to a fence. She has hold of the fence and in the companion piece (bottom) she is moving on beyond the fence.

152

Ruth in Her Garden. Designed and hooked by Liz Alpert Fay, Sandy Hook, Connecticut. 58" by 47".

"Ruth Spring lives in the Adirondack Mountains. She is an amazing woman and a great inspiration to me. Each Christmas I sit with Ruth by the wood stove at our family gatherings. I listen to her stories and try to absorb the vast amounts of knowledge she has to offer. Ruth is a long time organic gardener, landscape painter, and naturalist. Our holiday visits, and a visit to Ruth's garden last summer, were the inspiration for this rug."

Hooking Sweet Hooking. Hooked by Melonie Bushey, Vergennes, Vermont. 30" by 24". Designed by Beverly Conway Designs.

Hooking Sweet Hooking. Hooked by Davey DeGraff, Hinesburg, Vermont. 30" by 24". Designed by Beverly Conway Designs.

Hooking Sweet Hooking. Hooked by Evelyn Lawrence, Hallstead, Pennsylvania. 28" by 35". Designed by Beverly Conway Designs.

When I Am Old. Designed and hooked by Carol Morris Petillo, Vinalhaven, Maine. 37" by 24". "I love bright colors – reds and purples are my favorites – and the hit-or-miss technique is one I enjoy a great deal. Hence, this rug, with a caricature of me in the middle. Inspired by Jenny Joseph's poem, 'Warning,' although I got the words wrong."

Butt First. Designed and hooked by Jean Barber, Burlington, Vermont. 24" by 18". "My husband, Tom, is the source of my 'humor rug.' He says I go through life 'butt first' because when I start doing one thing, I always see another that needs doing first. So of course I had to hook my rear view as I frantically dash about. I used spirals to show motion. My rug is nearly finished, but first…"

Garden Fairies #3. Designed and hooked by Donna Lee Beaudoin, Hinesburg, Vermont. 15" by 15". "This is my third fairy piece, inspired by the materials used and a love of fairies."

A Woman with Attitude. Hooked by Doris Beatty, Falmouth, Massachusetts. 25" by 22". Designed by Doris Beatty and drawn by Craig D'Amario.
"In the classroom of Dianne Phillips, I was inspired to create a design that was meaningful to me at this point of my life. I love to run and this design is my expression of running the famous Falmouth Road Race past Nobska Lighthouse, in the front of the pack (with my white hair)."

The Cello (at Madison Square Garden, of course!) Designed and hooked by Rae Reynolds Harrell, Hinesburg, Vermont. 60" by 33".
"This is the second in my series of women playing instruments in an orchestra. 25-27 rugs anticipated in the series when all are finished."

Angel of the Morning. Hooked by Priscilla Heininger, Shelburne, Vermont. 39" by 24". Designed by Beverly Conway Designs.
"This design makes me smile! Beverly has captured the way I feel upon awakening, and I can picture myself standing in a flowered bathrobe and bunny slippers, holding my coffee mug, and wondering how to face the day. The colors remind me of chenille bathrobes and bedspreads from childhood. I love the rug for its relevance and humor!"

My Vote is Peace. Designed and hooked by Rae Reynolds Harrell, Hinesburg, Vermont. 24" by 22". "In this political election year, I want my voice heard for peace for all peoples."

Noah. Designed and hooked by Diane Phillips, Fairport, New York. 12" by 13". "A group to which I belong decided to each do a 'Noah's Ark' rug. In my rug, I've shown Noah contemplating the task ahead of him. I was inspired by the portraits by Van Gogh."

Wash Day. Designed and hooked by Paige Osborn Stoep, Lyons, New York. 35" by 25".

Joe and His Girls. Designed and hooked by Laurie M. Sybertz, Kingston, Massachusetts. 32" by 43".
"This design was inspired by my husband, Joe, the beekeeper. Joe enjoys sitting and relaxing on his bench, watching the bees fly in and out of the hives. He hand crafted the copper peaked roofs on the hives. The blue hands are my dye gloves he uses when handling the bees. I started this rug with Jule Marie Smith at the Green Mountain Rug School in 2002."

Self Portrait at Age 10. Designed and hooked by Gwenn C. Smith, Lebanon, New Hampshire. 27" by 15".
"In my second childhood, I tried to rediscover the child in me, the mix of fabrics, the bow in my hair and that cowlick with a lock always standing up straight on the top of my head. I tried to tame it by snipping it but it didn't work."

Dinty Moore Cold From the Can. Designed and hooked by Susan Charbonneau, Kinderhook, New York. 18" by 19".
"This rug is adapted from a favorite photo of our son Adam 'dining' on cold beef stew straight from the can."

Grandchildren in Monument Valley. Designed and hooked by Dayne Sousa, Pinehurst, North Carolina. 27" by 36".
"Our son, Gary, and family vacationed in Arizona in 2003 and photographed special places. I decided this photo would make a great rug."

Graffiti Tango. Designed and hooked by Judith Dallegret, Montreal, Quebec, Canada. 44" by 36".
"This rug is a self portrait, a souvenir of my Argentine Tango dancing days. The scribbled graffiti border reads 'Sur Les Quais, Paris Tango, La Tangeuria' and it includes my collection of dancing shoes. It is a 'Woman with Attitude' rug where she finally gets to lead."

The Knitters. Hooked by Nancy Norton, Avon, Connecticut. 53" by 27". Designed by Mary Azarian.
"I love to knit and I love 'period' rugs and furnishings. When I saw part of this rug hooked by the Green Mountain Guild as a raffle prize at one of their shows, I was eager to make it! I decided I wanted to do the entire illustration titled, 'Symphony for the Sheep,' and was fortunate to receive permission from Mary Azarian to do so."

Baking Cookies with Granny. Designed and hooked by Carol M. Munson, Sunderland, Vermont. 35" by 22".
"My mother's backward chair technique made it possible for the grandchildren to help Granny roll out the cookie dough."

Scarlett. Hooked by Diane S. Learmonth, West Newton, Iowa. 24" by 19". Designed by George Kahnle for Hooked on the Creek.
"I love this pattern of Scarlett sitting in the hills in the rain smelling a flower. She was fun to hook, especially with Sharon Townsend coaching me."

Sorrow. Designed and hooked by Sharon L. Townsend, Altoona, Iowa. 28" by 25". "Trying to use my art to help cope with a family tragedy while combining arcs and geometric designs for an assigned project produced this piece."

Study War No More. Designed and hooked by Sharon L. Townsend, Altoona, Iowa. 28" by 22". "A portrait class, a gray flamingo seen on TV in Iraq, and anger, all came together to make this rug. The shape is a skewed pentagon."

Right:
Franny the Flower Lady. Designed and hooked by Sharon L. Townsend, Altoona, Iowa. 17" by 7". "Franny is one in a series of bottle covers I'm doing for a mini class I'm teaching in Decorah, Iowa. She is a flower seller, the spring lady, come to Vermont to show her wares."

Snowman with Flamingo, a Pillow.
Hooked by Margery Kimpton,
Dunstable, Massachusetts. 21" by 11".
Designed by Beverly Conway Designs.

Right:
Winter in Michigan.
Hooked by Laura
Podob, Farmington
Hills, Michigan. 26"
by 19". Designed by
Molly E. Bond.
"This rug was
adapted from a
drawing by my ten-
year-old niece, Molly
Bond. I love how
Molly is holding the
carrot to go on the
snowman. I love
taking children's
drawings and turning
them into rugs."

Snowman With Broom Ornament.
Designed and hooked by Joann
Gochinski, South Deerfield, Massachusetts. 8" by 3".
"Being so terrible at drawing, I could
handle a snowman, but didn't like it
looking so flat so I added 3-D details
where I could."

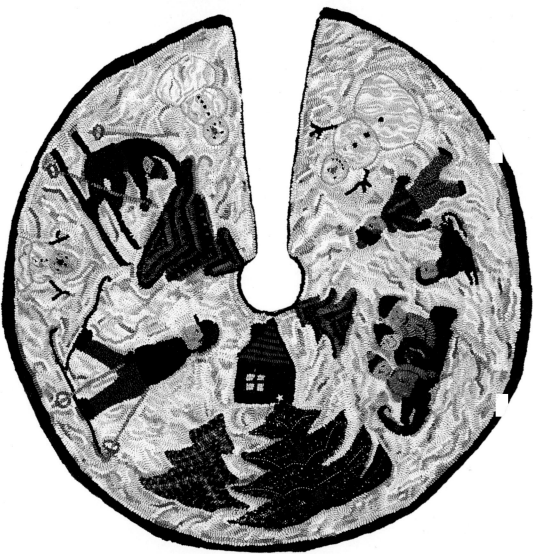

Winter Mishaps. Designed and hooked by Suzanne Dirmaier, Waterbury Center, Vermont. 41" diameter.
"I was enrolled in a primitive pictorial class that I was not prepared for. I sketched out a winter scene for a Christmas
tree skirt that I thought might do. I had hopes of a Scandinavian ski instructor named Swen who turned out to be
Bob in a red cap. The little boys look like they are careening toward an uncalculated end. The snowmen appear
from nowhere."

Children at Play. Hooked by Jean Evans, Pawlet, Vermont. 34" by 26".
Designed by Patsy Becker.
"This rug was made for Abigail Sciegaj, one of my ten grandchildren. I have
made rugs for all of them."

Dove of Peace Ornament. Hooked by Joann M.
Gochinski, South Deerfield, Massachusetts. 6" by 7".
Designer unknown.

Christmas Village. Hooked by Jeanne Laplante,
Burlington, Vermont. 46" diameter. Designed by
Jeanne Laplante and daughter, Louise.

Flying Santa. Hooked by Deb
Thomann, Gardner, Massachusetts.
14" by 18". Designer unknown.

162

Giving Thanks. Hooked by Tom McNerney, Newburyport, Massachusetts. Designed by Tom McNerney and Gull Cottage Rugs.
"The design started with the turkey from *Needle Love Magazine*. The rest came from my own love of Thanksgiving and all of its motifs."

Colin's Santa. Hooked by Cynthia Rotoli, Manchester, New Hampshire. 12" by 9". Designed by Colin Reade.
"Colin Reade is my amazing seven-year-old artist friend who drew this Santa for his sixth Christmas. He really wanted to learn to hook and this was our first project together. He lost interest in the hooking part (after many tries) but not in the finished piece. Color choices were his and different than the original (the green suit was the exception) and design decisions were mine."

Boo! Designed and hooked by Deborah Walsh, Cranford, New Jersey. 25" by 33".
"This is the first rug I designed – during a dye and design class with Dick and George at Shelburne. My inspiration was the old primitive Halloween decorations, and I added the candy corn to the borders because my three children were 'hooked' on candy corn during Halloween season while I hooked this rug."

Welcome to the North Pole. Hooked by Beverly J. Delnicki, Wheelock, Vermont. 62" by 49". Designed by Piece O'Cake Designs.
"After making 'Welcome to the North Pole' twice as quilts and giving them to my kids, it was time for one to keep. I give quilts – I keep rugs. The more you start to embellish, the more ways you find to add more."

Friendship Rug. Hooked by Anne Frost, Isle of Palms, South Carolina. 31" by 23". Designed by Judy Quintman, Elizabeth Morgan, Suzi Prather, Gail Schmidt, and Anne Frost.
"This is a friendship rug. Each square is designed and hooked by a different person. We are five friends, from different states, who meet once a year to attend a workshop together."

Friendship Rug. Hooked by Gail Schmidt, Little Silver, New Jersey. 30" by 22". Designed by Judy Quintman, Elizabeth Morgan, Suzi Prather, Gail Schmidt, and Anne Frost.
"A group of five women who met through rug hooking and developed a wonderful friendship decided to design and hook a friendship rug for one another."

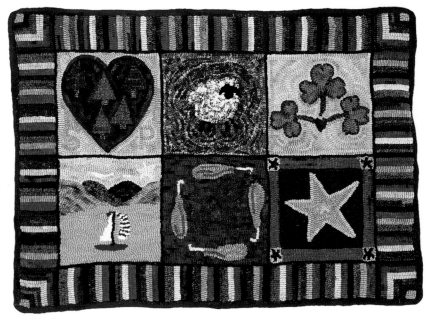

Friendship Rug. Hooked by Suzi Prather, Orlando, Florida. 30" by 22". Designed by Judy Quintman, Elizabeth Morgan, Suzi Prather, Gail Schmidt, and Anne Frost.
"The five of us 'hooking friends' from all over the United States pick a rug school each year to go to and catch up on each other's lives. This rug commemorates The Green Mountain Rug School. Hooking is a great way to meet and keep new friends."

Friendship Rug. Hooked by Judy Quintman, Wilmington, North Carolina. 30" by 23". Designed by Judy Quintman, Elizabeth Morgan, Suzi Prather, Gail Schmidt, and Anne Frost. "Five of us decided to commemorate our friendship, found through rug hooking, by doing a rug with blocks representative of each of us."

Kindred Spirit. Hooked by Donna Andrews Stefanik, Westfield, Massachusetts. 21" by 10". Designed by Vermont Folk Rugs.
"My kindred spirit would have to love color! She will hang in my studio!"

Friendship Rug. Hooked by Elizabeth Morgan, Wallingford, Vermont. 30" by 22". Designed by Judy Quintman, Elizabeth Morgan, Suzi Prather, Gail Schmidt, and Anne Frost.
"The five of us met at a rug camp, became friends, and decided to do a friendship rug. We are still attending rug camps together every year!"

Big Foot Angel. Hooked by Fiona Cooper Fenwick, Hinesburg, Vermont. 35" by 27". Designed by George Kahnle for Hooked on the Creek.

Guardian Angels. Hooked by Nancy D. Jewett, Pittsford, Vermont. 28" by 41". Designed by Nancy D. Jewett for Fluff & Peachy Bean Designs.
"A tribute to my mother-in-law, who taught me to hook. A few days before she died on June 5, 2000 she said, 'I love you all. If I should die, I'll come back as an angel to help all of you.' My mother-in-law and her beloved cat watching over us."

Gardening Angel. Hooked by Ann Berezowski, Bomoseen, Vermont. 11" by 18". Designed by Laurice Heath.

Memories. Designed and hooked by Tina Payton, Mexico, Maine. 21" by 36".
"As a teenager, I lost my mother. After nearly thirty years, it remains difficult for me to visit my mother's grave site without much sadness. After reading a book on gravestone rubbings, I became inspired to honor my mother's life by adapting one of the rubbings into my 'Memories' rug. Thanks to our early ancestors, a hook and some wool, I'm now able to visit these memories daily, with much happiness."

Skybound. Hooked by Brenda C. Williams, Valatie, New York. 61" by 23". Designed by Barbara Carroll.

Patriotic

God Bless America. Designed and hooked by Sue Hammond, New London, New Hampshire. 31" by 43".
"This was designed and named in the aftermath of 9/11, and made as a demonstration project while artisan-in-residence at Enfield Shaker Museum, Enfield, New Hampshire."

Tall Ships. Hooked by Sandra Town, Barre, Vermont. 32" by 26". Designed by Edana Pattern.

Nantucket. Designed and hooked by Davey DeGraff, Hinesburg, Vermont. 30" by 24".
"This design was inspired by a photo of an antique sailor whirligig."

The Healing. Designed and hooked by Melissa Van Marter-Rexford, South Hero, Vermont. 32" by 39".
"My love for the American Flag and all that it stands for sent me hooking Old Glory. I began this rug (my first full-sized) in July 2001. By the beginning of September 2001 I had hooked the field of stars and a few stripes. In the weeks following September 11, I finished the flag and the border was born. The 37 stars represent the remaining states and the unity of our nation during a time of healing."

Lady Liberty. Designed and hooked by Cherylyn Brubaker, Brunswick, Maine. 41" by 33".
"I wanted to design a patriotic pattern and was very taken with palindromes – words or phrases that read the same left to right as well as right to left."

Geometric Star. Hooked by Elizabeth Morgan, Wallingford, Vermont. 70" by 70". Design adapted by George Kahnle for Hooked on the Creek.
"This rug design is adapted from an antique rug that recently sold at auction for $46,000. It was designed as a square-sized rug, but I decided to take off the four corners and create a different shape."

Sgt. 1st Class Mike McGovern of the 40th Army Band. Designed and hooked by Trish Walden, Topsham, Vermont. 20" by 20".
"When the theme of our show was 'Stars and Stripes Forever,' I did a portrait of John Phillip Sousa. Mike admired it so much that I did a portrait of him for his retirement from the 40th Army Band, Vermont National Guard. During his membership in the Guards, as a trumpet player, Mike played taps at more than eight hundred funerals in Vermont, as well as concerts and parades."

America. Hooked by Nancy Urbanak, Cornwall, Vermont. 48" by 21". Designed by Beverly Conway Designs.
"I saw this rug partially hooked and loved it. I added the swirls in the sky to give it a more whimsical look."

A Towne Garden. Hooked by Kim Dubay, North Yarmouth, Maine. 31" by 32". Designed by Karen Kahle and Primitive Spirit.

Abundant Towne Garden. Hooked by Susan Mackey, Tinmouth, Vermont. 30" by 40". Designed by Karen Kahle and Primitive Spirit.

Abundant Towne Garden. Hooked by Robyn Hodges, Topsfield, Massachusetts. 30" by 40". Designed by Karen Kahle and Primitive Spirit.
"I was inspired to do this design by Karen Kahle after taking her class at last year's Hooked in the Mountains Rug School."

A Towne Garden. Hooked by Mary Hulette, South Burlington, Vermont. 31" by 32". Designed by Karen Kahle and Primitive Spirit.
"This rug was a wedding shower gift for Annie Burton, daughter of my dear friend, Debbie Burton. Annie was married in July 2003 to Matt Colaluca in Grand Isle. Annie and Matt now live in Colorado."

My Garden Shed. Designed and hooked by Kathleen Patten, Hinesburg, Vermont. 15" by 23".
"When I designed this rug it was the depth of winter. I stared at the mountains of snow and imagined what my garden shed looked like in the summer."

Folk Art House. Hooked by Andra Mollica, Brookfield, Connecticut. 29" by 16". Designer unknown.
"Adaptation of an antique rug from *American Hooked and Sewn Rugs: Folk Art Underfoot*, by Joel and Kate Kopp. I loved the colors in this rug and seem to love to hook houses. I have plans to hook my own home and property in one of my next rugs."

Saint John Motif #1. Designed and hooked by Melanie Coulson, Burlington, Vermont. 20" by 18".

Red Barn with Birches. Hooked by Betty Bouchard, Richmond, Vermont. 19" by 26". Designed by Maryanne Lincoln.
"Not long after a friend gave me a red woolen coat, I found Maryanne's design on sale at Dorr Woolen Mill. The coat couldn't have been a better choice for the barn. It was quality wool with a subtle check, which hooked up beautifully. I used it 'as is' except for a portion where I bled out some color. I dyed for the sky but everything else was 'as is' recycled wool."

Friendship Rug. Designed and hooked by Terri Cronin, Norwalk, Connecticut. 24" by 24".
"Also hooked by members of my rug hooking group."

My Grandmother's House. Designed and hooked by Pandy Goodbody, Williamstown, Massachusetts. 39" by 25".
"Happy summers spent at my grandmother's house in Sackets Harbor, New York inspired this rug. The sheep and hollyhocks are my addition, the pink horse chestnut tree used to be white. The black metal fence kept three little girls safe – how we longed to escape!"

Lizzie's Sugar House. Designed and hooked by Suzi Prather, Orlando, Florida. 40" by 28".
"This rug was inspired by a photo I took early one fall morning in Elizabeth Morgan's backyard. A train would go by a couple of times a week (not a steam engine) and she did have beautiful sunflowers."

George School - A Community of Friends. Designed and hooked by Claudia Casebolt, Lawrenceville, New Jersey. 26" by 40".
"This rug was hooked to celebrate my daughter Sahale's 2003 high school graduation from George School, a Quaker school in Newtown, Pennsylvania."

Lizzie's Sugar House. Hooked by Elizabeth Morgan, Wallingford, Vermont. 38" by 23".
Designed by Suzi Prather.
"Suzi took a picture of my sugar house and designed a wonderful Vermont pictorial."

The Garden at 21 Green Street. Designed and hooked by Gwenn C. Smith, Lebanon, New Hampshire. 19" by 26".
"It was a beautiful small garden that always had plants blooming. Even in winter, it was alive with snow-covered forms. I sold this house last November and this reminds me of my glorious garden in all its beauty. I shall miss it."

English Cottage Garden. Designed and hooked by Toni Philbrick, Hampden, Maine. 25" by 17".
"I designed this rug for a workshop doing a 'story' rug. It was inspired by my trip to England visiting gardens. I combined the concept of a Cotswald cottage, the sheep, and a beautiful garden that I planted and replanted several times!"

174

My Kentucky Home. Designed and hooked by Angela Jones, Raywick, Kentucky. 30" by 19".
"Living in Kentucky, horses, old homes, and wildflowers inspired me to design and hook this rug."

At Home in an Orchard. Designed and hooked by Sherillee Baker, Winterport, Maine. 26" by 21".

"I have been intrigued and excited by pictorials I've seen at the Green Mountain Rug Hooking Guild shows as well as those I've viewed in *Rug Hooking Magazine*. As I was preparing to attend a class in pictorials, I was inspired to depict the love of my home and its surrounding orchard by painting it in wool."

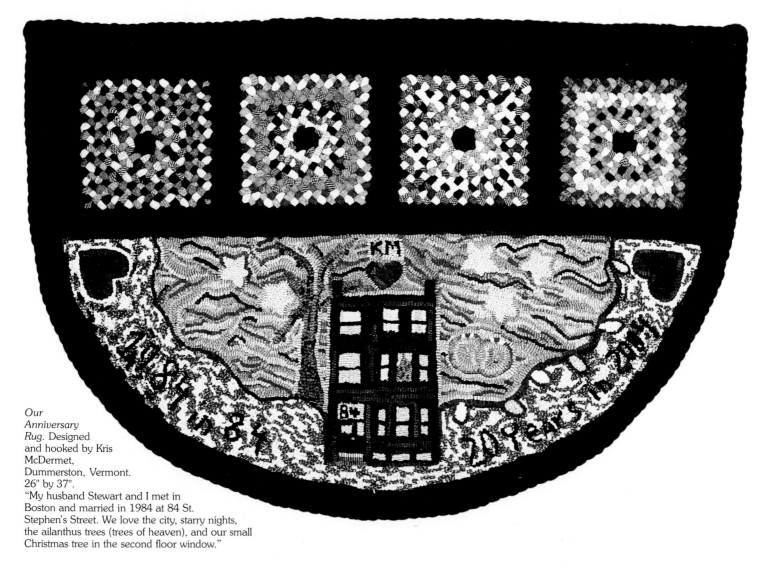

Our Anniversary Rug. Designed and hooked by Kris McDermet, Dummerston, Vermont. 26" by 37".

"My husband Stewart and I met in Boston and married in 1984 at 84 St. Stephen's Street. We love the city, starry nights, the ailanthus trees (trees of heaven), and our small Christmas tree in the second floor window."

The Till Place. Designed and hooked by Cheryl Dulong-Wasielewski, Greenfield, Massachusetts. 46" by 26".
"Over the past two and a half years my brother has seen rugs I've done for others and has no idea I've made one (at last) for him! I want to give this to my brother Thomas Till, and his wife Mary Lou for their 43rd anniversary. P.S. He's now contemplating adding on to their house yet again!"

Three Churches Mahone Bay. Hooked by Margaret Burggren, Amherst, Massachusetts. 16" by 20". Designed by Mary Doig.
"I picked up this design on a vacation to wonderful Mahone Bay."

Fruitlands. Hooked by Donna Lee Beaudoin, Hinesburg, Vermont. 32" by 38". Designed by Karen Kahle and Primitive Spirit.

Mountain Village. Hooked by Diana M. Link, Danby, Vermont. 36" by 18".
Design adapted by Diana M. Link from a quilted wall hanging.
"My first hooked rug adapted from a quilt pattern."

Old Stoney with Geraniums. Designed and hooked by Janet
Santaniello, Watchung, New Jersey. 43" by 26".
"'Hook your favorite things.' Old stone farmhouses are my most
favorite of things and geraniums are my favorite flower. This
combination has proven very successful for me. The rug was
chosen to be in *Celebration XII.* How lucky can you get?"

Twilight in Vermont. Designed
and hooked by Betty Bouchard,
Richmond, Vermont. 20" by 27".
"This farm in Richmond is a
natural setting for a picture. An
artist niece did a watercolor
painting of it as a gift to me. My
hooked version is quite different. I
chose to do it in autumn. Driving
home one evening I saw a sky I
just had to hook so I dyed and
incorporated it in this piece. The
rest is recycled wool."

My Cottage Garden. Hooked by Maureen Rowe, Dollard-Des-Ormeaux, Quebec, Canada. 36" by 27". Designed by Bluenose. "To me, flowers are the most feminine aspect in all of nature, encompassing all the life cycles. As a child, I wanted to be a farmer's wife living close to nature when I grew up. Now, living in the city, hooking flowers next to my dream cottage is the next best thing."

1394 Maple, Shawinigan. Designed and hooked by Louise G. de Tonnancour, Brossard, Quebec, Canada. 35" by 26".
"After the death of my parents, I felt a profound desire to go back to my roots on Maple Street in Shawinigan. The house where I was raised was the inspiration for this rug. Fond memories are attached to it. The border is a reminder of the way, as a kid, I admired how my mom, who loved to cook, would finish the edges of pies...especially apple pies."

The Animals Are Out. Hooked by Barbara Holt Hussey, Hinsdale, New Hampshire. 21" by 34". Designed by Deanne Fitzpatrick.
"This was my first completed rug. I was inspired by Deanne Fitzpatrick and my many trips to Nova Scotia with my husband. Our cat, Casper, and Belgian sheepdog, Mat, were personal additions."

Faith of Our Mothers. Designed and hooked by Emily Robertson, Falmouth, Massachusetts. 46" by 50".
"The house across the street from me formed the beginning of this composition. The bare tree branches added interest. I added the pine tree, church, and fence to complete the pictorial."

Gurnet Light. Designed and hooked by Olga Rothschild, Duxbury, Massachusetts. 38" by 28".
"The design was inspired by a local lighthouse that is much loved and landlocked."

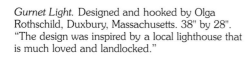

Primitive Pictorial (with modifications). Hooked by Mary Pringle, South Hero, Vermont. 44" by 21". Designed by Vermont Folk Rugs.

The Vermont State House. Designed and hooked by Stephanie Krauss for Green Mountain Hooked Rugs, Montpelier, Vermont. 24" by 34".

"The state house in Montpelier, Vermont is the central gathering place in the town and surrounding area. It's not just a political rally that draws people, but summer band concerts, holiday festivals, and fireworks. Children and adults alike flock to the large green for a game of ball or Frisbee and when the snow flies, you'll see happy sledding parties. I've passed by this place almost every day I have lived in Montpelier so I thought it would be fun to study the state house by hooking it in a rug."

Reconstruction. Hooked by Janet Carruth, Phoenix, Arizona. 30" by 45". Designed by W. Cushing and Company and Janet Carruth.

"Having never seen a hooked rug except in magazines, and knowing no one who hooked, I struggled to teach myself. Some time later a trio of hooking teachers traveled to Arizona and taught an intensive workshop. Using the basic outline or 'blueprint' of the houses as starting points, I totally changed the inside design to reflect the person I am today and the 'hot' colors I wanted to use. Teacher Bev Conway helped to make my vision a reality. The final outcome wasn't just a restoration of the old original houses. It was more like a reconstruction."

Washington's Birth Place. Hooked by Susan Longchamps, West Burke, Vermont. 35" by 25". Designed by Joan Moshimer.
"One of my favorite designs I had saved until I could use some of my first dyed yards of wool."

Home 1994. Designed and hooked by DonnaSue Shaw, Grand Isle, Vermont. 34" by 31".
"In 1994, we built a huge addition onto our little house. My parents and grandmother came to live with my husband, myself, and our four sons. We have enjoyed multigenerational living ever since. I designed and hooked this rug in memory of my grandmother, who passed away in 2002. Our initials create the border."

180

Welcome

Faith and Hope. Designed and hooked by Roberta Brewster, Saranac Lake, New York. 24" by 36".
"I am a decorative painter. Often I work with folk art designs. This rug is a takeoff on one of the designs I paint."

Skiers & Hookers Welcome. Designed and hooked by Norma Batastini, Glen Ridge, New Jersey. 16" by 26".
"Visitors to our Vermont mountain home are usually skiers or hookers, so a welcome rug in their honor inspired this rug. The background was hooked from a recycled woman's suit from the sixties. It was perfect for a snowy winter sky."

Welcome!! Designed and hooked by Burma Cassidy, Rochester, Vermont. 28" by 13".
"This is a bright happy sign to welcome all into my home. I loved working with the reds. I was inspired by Chuck Close's use of small squares of colored geometrics, so I played around with them. They remind me of confetti at a parade!"

Pussy Willow Welcome. Hooked by Marilou Leclaire, Clemons, New York. 38" by 20". Designed by Yankee Peddler Design.
"After a few classes, this was one of my first attempts at shading realistic flowers."

Three Cats. Hooked by Joann M. Gochinski, South Deerfield, Massachusetts. 36" by 18". Designed by DiFranza Designs.
"This is my second rug but my first completed rug. Started in October 2003 and finished February 2004."

Welcome Friends. Hooked by Melissa Van Marter-Rexford, South Hero, Vermont. 22" by 37". Designed by Marion Ham – Quail Hill Designs.
"This pattern came in a box of stuff I purchased four years ago when I was a new hooker. 'Someday I'll be able to hook this' were my thoughts. Someday is here and by God's grace, I have this gift. My love to my husband, Craig, and son, Rudd (who loves to cut my wool) for their never-ending patience while I hooked madly for this show. To Gwen Kjelleran, my dear friend and teacher, my life has forever changed. Thanks for getting me hooked!"

Pineapple Welcome. Designed and hooked by Norma Batastini, Glen Ridge, New Jersey. 18" by 13".
"I came to Abby Vakay's multimedia class with my pineapple pattern, not knowing what to expect. Wow, did she open our eyes to many new techniques and materials! Needle felting caught my fancy and fit right in with the personality of the pineapple. I'll never hook another rug without stopping to think, 'what if?'"

Welcome. Hooked by Shirley H. Zandy, Tinmouth, Vermont. 25" by 30". Designed by Karen Kahle and Primitive Spirit.

Wedding Rug. Designed and hooked by Polly S. Alexander, Essex Junction, Vermont. 35" by 26".
"This rug is a wedding gift for my niece and her husband. Their recent interest in antiques inspired this primitive 'lovebird' design."

Nova Scotia. Designed and hooked by Janice Peyton, Excello, Missouri. 17" by 25".
"Dana Sidwa and Jeremy Cooper Wedding. June 28, 2003.
Margaretsville Lighthouse, Fundy Bay, Nova Scotia.
Life goes on as usual (fisherman on the pier and town cat scavenging for dinner).
Lobster (120 served – my first).
Little red boat kept a silent watch!
Fish Shack (Artist Circle) provided two original water color souvenirs.
Beautiful wild lupins everywhere (wedding bouquets).
"Nova Scotia" – our honeymoon – just 46 years late!"

Wedding Rug. Hooked by Willy Cochran, Jericho, Vermont. 32" by 22". Designed by Patsy Becker.
"This design was adapted to include marriage information for my granddaughter."

Colin and Carrie's Wedding Rug. Designed and hooked by Mary Lee O'Connor, Ballston Spa, New York. 26" by 18".

Cindy and Maurice's Marriage Rug. Designed and hooked by Gail Duclos Lapierre, Shelburne, Vermont. 25" by 21".
"This rug was made in celebration of the marriage of Cynthia Johnson and Maurice DuBois II. Freddie the cat is an important part of the family. He's in the window looking out for them."

Caleb and Leah's Wedding Rug. Designed and hooked by Kathleen Patten, Hinesburg, Vermont. 53" by 41".
"Davey DeGraff made a rug for her son's wedding. That inspired me to make a rug for my son. They will stand on it to be married May 29, 2004. This is their house on Vermont Avenue in Washington D.C."

Chapter 8

Bags and Purses

Red Flowers Purse. Designed and hooked by Rita Barnard, Ann Arbor, Michigan. 10" by 6".

Dogwood Tote Bag. Hooked by Lois Johnstone, Wallingford, Vermont. 20" by 14". Designed by Beverly Conway Designs.

Spring Dew. Designed and hooked by Donna Lee Beaudoin, Hinesburg, Vermont. 11" by 11".
"This was a practice piece done in Amy Oxford's class. These are Amy's Broken Rules."

Winter Shoulder Bag. Designed and hooked by Gail Majauckas, West Newbury, Massachusetts. 11" by 14".
"Number 1 in a series of seasonal shoulder bags."

Pendleton Shirt Purse. Hooked by Gail Duclos Lapierre, Shelburne, Vermont. 8" by 8". Designed by Nola Heidbreder.
"Last year I took Nola's purse class. I shared a table with Nancy Zickler. When we started our Pendleton shirt purses, we used some of each other's shirts in our purses. Tragically, Nancy died in a house fire shortly before Christmas. I had set the unfinished purse aside after the class, but made sure I had it finished for this year's show for her."

Red Bag. Designed and hooked by Burma Cassidy, Rochester, Vermont. 12" by 11".
"I hooked these stars and sewed them onto an 'as is' bag."

Victorian Purse. Designed and hooked by Donna Lee Beaudoin, Hinesburg, Vermont. 11" by 10".
"This purse was inspired by velvet and the sparkly gold. This was not a planned project, it just evolved."

At the Green Mountain Rug Hooking Guild's 2003 spring meeting, guild members divided up into teams and were given the challenge of creating a purse. The following bags are a result of this challenge.

Hooker's Case. Designed and hooked by Sandy Marquis, Polly Alexander, and Elizabeth Morgan. 6" by 8" (18" by 8" when open).

Untitled Purse. Designed and hooked by Barbara Held, Jule Marie Smith, and Rae Harrell. 7" by 9".
"Many creative minds and hands contributed to the final design. The purse was finished by Barbara Held."

Golden Crown Shoulder Bag. Designed and hooked by Burma Cassidy, Susan Mackey, and Gloria Reynolds. 9" by 8".

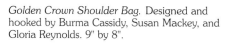

Envelope Purse. Designed and hooked by Shirley H. Zandy, Helen Wolfel, Priscilla Buzzell, and Anne-Marie Littenberg. 6" by 6". This bag was chosen as the "winner" by Shelburne Museum staff and curators who judged the outcome of the various hand-bag teams' efforts.

Rug Show Vendors

The following vendors exhibited at Hooked in the Mountains IX. They are an important part of our rug show, and our community, providing the finest materials, outstanding patterns, mouthwatering wools, and as always, lots of greatly-valued advice, assistance, and inspiration. The show wouldn't be the same without them and they are listed here as excellent resources for hooked rug enthusiasts.

To The Wool. Hooked by Dick LaBarge, Victory Mills, New York. 47" by 13". Designed by George Kahnle for Hooked on the Creek. At the rug show, this rug hung appropriately at the top of a stairway, pointing to the bottom level of the round barn, where the many vendors sold their wares and, of course, their wool.
"From a Shaker type antique sign that led visitors to their community, 'To The Gate.' We thought a wool dealer could have many of their wools represented in their sign so they could just point to the hooked color/texture when asked, 'How does it hook up?'"

American Country
Lucille Festa
52 Kent Road
Wilton, CT 06897
(203) 762-7595
lucillefesta@hotmail.com

Beaver Brook Crafts
Nancy Urbanak
1235 Sperry Road
Cornwall, VT 05753
(802) 462-2557

Beverly Conway Designs
Beverly Conway
1859 Munger Street
Middlebury, VT 05753
(802) 388-7742
prism@together.net

The Dorr Mill Store
Terry Dorr
P.O. Box 88
Guild, NH 03754
(800) 846-3677
www.dorrmillstore.com

Susan Gingras – Baskets
3004 Snake Mountain Road
Weyridge, VT 05753
(802) 545-2672

Green Mountain Hooked Rugs
Stephanie Krauss
146 Main Street
Montpelier, Vermont 05602
(802) 223-1333
www.GreenMountainHookedRugs.com

Rae Harrell Rug Hooking Studio
Rae Harrell
154 Mallard Pond
Hinesburg, VT 05461
(802) 482-2076
raeharrell@gmavt.net

Heart in Hand Rug Hooking
Norma Batastini
P.O. Box 8117
Glenn Ridge, NJ 07028
(973) 746-5361

Heavens to Betsy
Betsy Reed
46 Route 23
Claverack, NY 12513
(518) 851-2149
Reed1@mhcable.com

Hooked Treasures
Cherylyn Brubaker
6 Iroquois Circle
Brunswick, ME 04011
(207) 729-1380
www.hookedtreasures.com

Kinderhook B & B
Jayne Hester
67 Broad Street
Kinderhook, NY 12106
(518) 758-1850
kinderhookb-b@berk.com

Liziana Creations
Diana O'Brien and Liz O'Brien
P.O. Box 59
South Windsor, CT 06074
(860) 290-8619
diana@galaxy.net
www.liziana.com

Primitive Spirit
Karen Kahle
445 West 19th
Eugene, OR 97401
(541) 344-4316
k_rathbun@hotmail.com
www.primitivespiritrugs.com

Rug Hooking Magazine
Virginia P. Stimmel – Editor
1300 Market Street, Suite 202
Lemoyne, PA 17043
(717) 234-5091
www.rughookingonline.com

Rug Wool Studio
Judy Kohler
401 Shelly Hill Road
Stanfordville, NY 12581
(845) 266-4112
judy@rugwoolstudio.com
www.rugwoolstudio.com

The Singing Bird
Arlene Scanlon
18 South Hill Drive
Essex Junction, VT 05452
(802) 878-5917

Membership Information

The Green Mountain Rug Hooking Guild began in 1981 when a group of dedicated rug hookers from Vermont decided to form a guild. Their purpose was to make it possible to meet twice a year, to share their joy of rug hooking, and to learn from each other and outside speakers.

New guild members receive a packet of information, which includes a full membership list, by-laws, a teacher and supplier list, and the most recent newsletter. We are able to provide a listing of members in their immediate area and can refer them to representatives and teachers. Our newsletter keeps everyone current because many are unable to attend the fall and spring meetings.

To join the guild, please visit our web site at:
www.greenmountainrughookingguild.org.

Dues are $15.00 for members of ATHA (Association of Traditional Hooking Artists) or $17.00 for non-ATHA members. If you would like to become a member, but are unable to visit our web site, please send a check or money order for your dues (payable to Green Mountain Rug Hooking Guild, Inc.), along with your name, address, city, state, zip code, phone number, and email address to:

Patty Yoder
499 Merrill Spring Rd.
Tinmouth, VT 05773
802-446-3162
yoyo@vermontel.net

Thank you for joining or renewing your membership to the guild.

Suggested Reading

Books

Allard, Mary. *Rug Making: Techniques and Design.* Philadelphia, Pennsylvania: Chilton Book Company, 1963.

Aller, Doris. *Handmade Rugs.* Menlo Park, California: Lane Publishing Company, c. 1953.

Batchelder, Martha. *The Art of Hooked-Rug Making.* Peoria, Illinois: The Manual Arts Press, 1947.

Beatty, Alice, and Mary Sargent. *Basic Rug Hooking.* Harrisburg, Pennsylvania: Stackpole Books, 1990.

Beatty, Alice, and Mary Sargent. *The Hook Book.* Harrisburg, Pennsylvania: Stackpole Books, 1977.

Boswell, Thom, ed. *The Rug Hook Book: Techniques, Projects and Patterns for This Easy, Traditional Craft.* New York: Sterling Publishing Co., Inc., 1992.

Bramlett, Carol, and Leslie Hoy. *A Celebration of Hand-Hooked Rugs VIII.* Edited by Patrice A. Crowley. Harrisburg, Pennsylvania: Stackpole Books, 1998.

Burton, Mary Sheppard. *A Passion for the Creative Life: Textiles to Lift the Spirit.* Edited by Mary Ellen Cooper. Germantown, Maryland: Sign of the Hook Books, 2002.

A Celebration of Hand-Hooked Rugs. Harrisburg, Pennsylvania: Stackpole Books, 1991.

Cooper, Mary Ellen, ed. *A Celebration of Hand-Hooked Rugs II.* Harrisburg, Pennsylvania: Stackpole Books, 1992.

Cooper, Mary Ellen, ed. *A Celebration of Hand-Hooked Rugs III.* Harrisburg, Pennsylvania: Stackpole Books, 1993.

Crouse, Gloria E. *Hooking Rugs: New Materials, New Techniques* (and companion video). Newtown, Connecticut: The Taunton Press, 1990.

Crowley, Patrice A., ed. *A Celebration of Hand-Hooked Rugs V.* Harrisburg, Pennsylvania: Stackpole Books, 1995.

Crowley, Patrice A., ed. *A Celebration of Hand-Hooked Rugs VI.* Harrisburg, Pennsylvania: Stackpole Books, 1996.

Crowley, Patrice A., ed. *A Celebration of Hand-Hooked Rugs VII.* Harrisburg, Pennsylvania: Stackpole Books, 1997.

Crowley, Patrice A., ed. *A Rug Hooker's Garden.* Harrisburg, Pennsylvania: Rug Hooking Magazine, 2000.

Davies, Ann. *Rag Rugs: How to Use Ancient and Modern Rug-Making Techniques to Create Rugs, Wallhangings, Even Jewelry – 12 Projects.* New York: Henry Holt and Company, Inc., 1992.

Davis, Mildred J. *The Art of Crewel Embroidery.* New York: Crown Publishing, 1962.

Davis, Mildred J. *Early American Embroidery Designs.* New York: Crown Publishing, 1969.

Davis, Mildred J., ed. *Embroidery Designs, 1780-1820; From the manuscript collection, The Textile Resource and Research Center, the Valentine Museum,* Richmond, Virginia. New York, Crown Publishing, 1971.

Eber, Dorothy H. *Catherine Poirier's Going Home Song.* Halifax, Nova Scotia: Nimbus Publishing, 1994.

Felcher, Cecelia. *The Complete Book of Rug Making: Folk Methods and Ethnic Designs.* New York: Hawthorne Books, 1975.

Field, Jeanne. *Shading Flowers: The Complete Guide for Rug Hookers.* Harrisburg, Pennsylvania: Stackpole Books, 1991.

Fitzpatrick, Deanne. *Hook Me A Story: The History and Method of Rug Hooking in Atlantic Canada.* Halifax, Nova Scotia: Nimbus Publishing, Ltd., 1999.

Halliwell, Jane E. *The Pictorial Rug: Everything You Need to Know to Hook a Realistic, Impressionistic, or Primitive Picture With Wool.* Rug Hooking Magazine's Framework Series 2000, Edition V. Lemoyne, Pennsylvania: M. David Detweiler, 2000.

Henry Ford Museum & Greenfield Village. *Edward Sands Frost's Hooked Rug Patterns.* Dearborn Michigan: Edison Institute, 1970.

Hoy, Leslie, and Sarah Wilt. *A Celebration of Hand-Hooked Rugs IX.* Edited by Patrice A. Crowley. Harrisburg, Pennsylvania: Stackpole Books, 1999.

Hoy, Leslie. *A Celebration of Hand-Hooked Rugs X.* Edited by Patrice A. Crowley. Harrisburg, Pennsylvania: Stackpole Books, 2000.

Hoy, Leslie. *A Celebration of Hand-Hooked Rugs XI.* Edited by Patrice A. Crowley. Lemoyne, Pennsylvania: Rug Hooking Magazine, 2001.

Hoy, Leslie. *A Celebration of Hand-Hooked Rugs XII.* Edited by Wyatt R. Myers. Lemoyne, Pennsylvania: Rug Hooking Magazine, 2002.

Johnson, Barbara. *American Classics: Hooked Rugs From the Barbara Johnson Collection.* Jenkintown, Pennsylvania. Squibb Corp., 1988.

Kennedy, MacDonald, ed. *A Celebration of Hand-Hooked Rugs IV.* Harrisburg, Pennsylvania: Stackpole Books, 1994.

Kent, William W. *The Hooked Rug.* New York: Tudor Publishing Company, 1930.

Kent, William W. *Hooked Rug Design.* Springfield, Massachusetts: The Pond-Ekberg Company, 1949.

Kent, William W. *Rare Hooked Rugs and Other: Both Antique & Modern.* Springfield, Massachusetts: The Pond-Ekberg Company, 1941.

Ketchum, William C., Jr. *Hooked Rugs: A Historical and Collectors Guide: How to Make Your Own.* New York: Harcourt, Brace, Jovanovich, 1976.

King, Mrs. Harry. *How To Hook Rugs.* Little Rock, Arkansas: D. P. and L. Company, 1948.

Kopp, Joel, and Kate Kopp. *American Hooked and Sewn Rugs: Folk Art Underfoot.* New York: E. P. Dutton, Inc., 1985.

Lais, Emma Lou, and Barbara Carroll. *Antique Colours for Primitive Rugs: Formulas Using Cushing Acid Dyes.* Kennebunkport, Maine: W. Cushing & Company, 1996.

Lais, Emma Lou, and Barbara Carroll. *American Primitive Hooked Rugs: Primer for Recreating Antique Rugs.* Kennebunkport, Maine: Wildwood Press, 1999.

Lawless, Dorothy. *Rug Hooking and Braiding For Pleasure and Profit.* New York: Thomas Y. Crowell, 1962.

Linsley, Leslie. *Hooked Rugs: An American Folk Art.* New York, New York: Clarkson N. Potter, Inc., 1992.

Logsdon, Roslyn. *People and Places: Roslyn Logsdon's Imagery In Fiber.* Rug Hooking Magazine's 1998 Framework Series Edition. Harrisburg, Pennsylvania: David Detweiler, 1998.

Mather, Anne D. *Creative Rug Hooking.* New York, New York: Sterling Publishing Company, 2000.

McGown, Pearl K. *Color in Hooked Rugs.* West Boylston, Massachusetts: Pearl K. McGown, 1954.

McGown, Pearl K. *The Lore and Lure of Hooked Rugs.* West Boylston, Massachusetts: Pearl K. McGown, 1966.

McGown, Pearl K. *Persian Patterns.* West Boylston, Massachusetts: Pearl K. McGown, 1958.

McGown, Pearl K. *You...Can Hook Rugs.* West Boylston, Massachusetts: Pearl K. McGown, 1951.

Minick, Polly and Laurie Simpson. *Folk Art Friends: Hooked Rugs and Coordinating Quilts.* Woodinville, Washington: Martingale and Company, 2003.

Montell, Joseph. *The Art of Speed Tufting.* Santa Ana, California: RC Rug Crafters, 1976.

Moshimer, Joan. *The Complete Rug Hooker: A Guide to the Craft.* Boston, Massachusetts: New York Graphic Society, 1975.

Moshimer, Joan. *Hooked on Cats: Complete Patterns and Instructions for Rug Hookers.* Harrisburg, Pennsylvania: Stackpole Books, 1991.

Myer, Wyatt, ed. *Basic Rug Hooking.* Lemoyne, Pennsylvania: Rug Hooking Magazine, 2002.

Myers, Lori. *A Celebration of Hand-Hooked Rugs XIII: The Finest of Fiber Art.* Edited by Wyatt R. Myers. Leymoyne, Pennsylvania: Rug Hooking Magazine, 2003.

Oxford, Amy. *Punch Needle Rug Hooking: Techniques and Designs.* Atglen, Pennsylvania: Schiffer Publishing Ltd., 2003.

Parker, Xenia L. *Hooked Rugs & Ryas: Designing Patterns and Applying Techniques.* Chicago, Illinois: Henry Regency Company, 1973.

Peladeau, Mildred C. *Art Underfoot: The Story of the Waldoboro Hooked Rugs.* Lowell, Massachusetts: American Textile History Museum, 1999.

Peverill, Sue. *Make Your Own Rugs: A Guide to Design and Technique.* London: Hamlyn Publishing Group, Ltd., 1989.

Phillips, Anna M. *Hooked Rugs and How to Make Them.* New York: Macmillan, 1925.

Ries, Estelle H. *American Rugs.* Cleveland, Ohio: The World Publishing Company, 1950.

Rex, Stella H. *Choice Hooked Rugs.* New York, New York: Prentice-Hall, 1953.

Rex, Stella H. *Practical Hooked Rugs.* Ashville, Maine: Cobblesmith, 1975.

A Rug Hooking Book of Days Featuring the Fiber Art of Polly Minick. Harrisburg, Pennsylvania: Stackpole Books, 1998.

Siano, Margaret, and Susan Huxley. *The Secrets of Finishing Hooked Rugs.* Lemoyne, Pennsylvania: Rug Hooking Magazine, 2003.

Stratton, Charlotte K. *Rug Hooking Made Easy.* New York: Harper and Brothers Publishers, 1955.

Taylor, Mary P. *How To Make Hooked Rugs.* Philadelphia: David McKay Company, c. 1930.

Tennant, Emma. *Rag Rugs of England and America.* London: Walker Books, 1992.

Turbayne, Jessie A. *Hooked Rugs: History and The Continuing Tradition.* West Chester, Pennsylvania: Schiffer Publishing, Ltd., 1991.

Turbayne, Jessie A. *Hooked Rug Treasury.* Atglen, Pennsylvania: Schiffer Publishing Ltd., 1997.

Turbayne, Jessie A. *The Hooker's Art.* Atglen, Pennsylvania: Schiffer Publishing Ltd., 1993.

Turbayne, Jessie A. *The Complete Guide to Collecting Hooked Rugs: Unrolling the Secrets.* Atglen, Pennsylvania: Schiffer Publishing Ltd., 2004.

Underhill, Vera B., and Arthur J. Burks. *Creating Hooked Rugs.* New York, New York: Coward-McCann, 1951.

Vail, Juju. *Rag Rugs: Techniques in Contemporary Craft Projects.* Edison, New Jersey: Chartwell Books, 1997.

Von Rosenstiel, Helene. *American Rugs and Carpets From the Seventeenth Century to Modern Times.* New York: Morrow, c. 1978.

Walch, Margaret, and Augustine Hope. *Living Colors: The Definitive Guide to Color Palettes Through the Ages.* San Francisco: Chronicle Books, 1995.

Waugh, Elizabeth. *Collecting Hooked Rugs.* New York, London: The Century Company, 1927.

Wilcox, Bettina. *Hooked Rugs for Fun and Profit, With Original Hooked Rugs, Designs and Patterns From Famous Museum Collections.* New York: Homecrafts, c.1949.

Wiseman, Ann. *Hand Hooked Rugs and Rag Tapestries.* New York: Van Nostrand Reinhold Company, Inc., 1969.

Yoder, Patty. *The Alphabet of Sheep.* Raleigh, North Carolina: Ivy House Publishing Group, 2003.

Yoder, Patty, ed. *Green Mountain Rug Hooking Guild Dye Book.* Tinmouth, Vermont: Green Mountain Rug Hooking Guild, 2003.

Young, Arthur. *America Gets Hooked: History of a Folk Art.* Lewiston, Maine: Booksplus, 1994.

Zarbok, Barbara J. *The Complete Book of Rug Hooking.* Princeton, New Jersey: D. Van Nostrand Company, Inc., 1961.

Periodicals

Rug Hooking Magazine, 1300 Market St., Suite 202, Lemoyne, PA 17043-1420

Fiberarts Magazine, Interweave Press, 201 E. Fourth St., Loveland, CO 80537-5655.

Piecework Magazine, Interweave Press, 201 E. Fourth St., Loveland, CO 80537-5655.

Index
(By Rug Hooker)

Aiken, Jill, 71, 92
Alain, Susan, 62, 137
Alexander, Polly S., 149, 183, 187
Andreson, Susan, 52, 71
Andrews-Maness, Donna, 146
Baker, Sherillee, 175
Balon, Karen, 24, 27
Barber, Jean, 154
Barbour, Kathie, 94
Barnard, Rita, 70, 73, 185
Barney, Carolyn, 84
Bartlett, Pam, 139
Batastini, Norma, 36, 181, 182
Beard, Jean W., 57
Beatty, Doris, 155
Beaudoin, Donna Lee, 154, 176, 186, 187
Becker, Patsy, 92
Becker, Trish, 103
Behrendt, Becky, 54, 95
Berezowski, Ann, 166
Bottjer, Marilyn, 121
Bouchard, Betty, 172, 177
Boudrieau, Debra, 88
Brana, Jean, 107
Breton, Sheila M., 42, 59, 143
Brewster, Roberta, 181
Brubaker, Cherylyn, 168
Bucceri, Loretta, 35
Burgess, Diane, 45
Burggren, Margaret, 176
Burghoff, Sara Jane, 70
Burnett, Kristina, 116
Bush, Judith B., 90, 117
Bushey, Melonie, 86, 99, 153
Buzzell, Priscilla, 36, 129, 188
Carruth, Janet, 180
Carter, Pamela, 3, 85
Casebolt, Claudia, 94, 173
Cassidy, Burma, 95, 100, 144, 148, 149, 150, 151, 181, 187, 188
Chaiken, Shirley, 49, 106, 144
Charbonneau, Susan, 71, 116, 138, 157
Ciemiewicz, Jon, 28, 81, 82, 106
Clarke, Jane B., 126, 148
Cochran, Willy, 183
Collins, Marion, 89
Connor, Cheryl, 58
Conway, Beverly, 63, 109
Cooper, Karen Baxter, 71, 78, 119
Coughlin, Linda Rae, 68
Coulson, Melanie, 172
Cronin, Terri, 73, 173
Cunningham, Penny, 147
Curtis, Kendra B., 67
D'Albora, Sally, 60
Dallegret, Judith, 60, 158
Danforth, Dot, 95
Davey, Jennifer, 34
Dawley, Barbara, 61
de Tonnancour, Louise G., 178
DeGraff, Davey, 31, 49, 104, 111, 153, 168
DeGregorio, Susan, 89
Delaney, Eugenie, 152
Delnicki, Beverly J., 61, 135, 163
Detrick, Karen, 82
Devlin, Kathy, 65
Dickie, Marion, 43
Dirmaier, Suzanne, 24, 25, 50, 161
Dodds, Judy B., 65
Doolittle, Lory, 77, 91
Dubay, Kim, 170
Dubois-Frey, Joan, 53
Ducharme, Sandy, 44
Dulong-Wasielewski, Cheryl, 105, 110, 176
Dye, Molly W., 48, 64, 100, 130
Egenes, Erika Anderson, 44

Ellingham, Nancy, 75, 121
English, Judith, 71, 83, 148
Erb, Rebecca, 80, 85, 124
Evans, Jean, 162
Fay, Liz Alpert, 153
Feller, Susan, 66, 67, 105
Fenwick, Fiona Cooper, 165
Ferdinando, Gail, 50, 96
Festa, Lucille B., 106, 118
Fraioli, Maddy, 63, 68
Frost, Anne, 164
Frost, Ruth, 114
Gage, Kathy, 107
Garcia, Robin, 43
Gault, Susan, 37, 38, 76
Gingras, Susan, 53, 93, 99, 104, 109
Gochinski, Joann M., 161, 162, 182
Goldsmith, Helena A., 62
Goodbody, Pandy, 93, 173
Gooding, Chris, 112, 113
Graf, Norma, 96
Griswold, Jane, 55
Guay, Mary, 106
Guindon, Jocelyn, 111, 129
Guth, Elizabeth, 132
Hall, Mary Ellen, 43
Hammond, Sue, 37, 89, 121, 167
Hansen, Jacqueline L., 91
Harrell, Rae Reynolds, 25, 155, 156, 188
Haskell, Evelyn, 46, 47, 58
Hautanen, Gloria, 40
Hebert, Joan, 108
Heidbreder, Nola A., 143
Heininger, Priscilla, 155
Heinlein, Eunice Whitney, 38, 123, 139
Held, Barbara, 48, 54, 147, 149, 188
Henderson, Joanna, 57
Henning, Cathy, 70, 79
Henning, Miriam, 36, 102, 103, 110, 125, 135
Hochman, Joelle, 80, 108
Hodges, Robyn, 170
House, Cindy, 75
Hulette, Mary, 51, 171
Hussey, Barbara Holt, 59, 178
Hutchins, Kathy, 103
Irish, Peg, 66, 67
Isabelle, Yvonne, 77
Jackson, Marilyn, 47
Jacobs, Rachel T., 97
Jamar, Tracy, 52
Jameson, Mary, 37, 115
Janssen, Sue, 140
Jensen, Kristi, 68
Jewett, Nancy D., 39, 166
Johnstone, Lois, 185
Jones, Angela, 175
Jose, Denise W., 137
Kahle, Karen, 42, 69, 76, 88, 93
Kaiser, Barbara, 103
Kaiser, Debra, 114
Kelley, Deb, 86, 117, 124, 135
Kelly, Diane, 65, 146
Kidder, Alan S., 84, 122, 128
Kimpton, Margery, 145, 161
Kirby, Debbie, 83
Kirouac, Sally W., 80
Kjelleren, Gwen, 131
Knight, Janet, 79
Koehler, Susan I., 42
Krauss, Stephanie A., 78, 180
LaBarge, Dick, 46, 145, 189
Labelle, Cyndi Melendy, 125
Lampe-Wilson, Susan, 123
Lapierre, Gail Duclos, 30, 126, 127, 184, 186

Laplante, Jeanne, 162
Lary, Bev, 128, 140
Laskowski, Jeri, 5, 60, 74, 78
Latham, Tony, 81, 129
Lathrop, Susan, 80
Laufer, Sharon, 107
Lavoie, Jen, 23, 29, 98, 107, 135
Lawrence, Evelyn, 86, 87, 118, 120, 127, 153
Learmonth, Diane S., 81, 113, 159
Leclaire, Marilou, 181
Liang, Coren Moore, 41, 45
Link, Diana M., 86, 111, 120, 177
Littenberg, Anne-Marie, 27, 30, 54, 124, 128, 132, 133, 134, 150, 188
Longchamps, Susan, 144, 180
Lowe, Sherry Craig, 101, 102
Ludwig, Barbara, 148
Mackey, Susan, 43, 170, 188
MacQuiddy, Jean, 145
Maddi-Perks, Karen L., 131
Madison, Sarah, 59
Majauckas, Gail, 116, 186
Manago, Noriko, 56
Marquis, Sandy, 187
Martin, Karen T., 65
McAdoo, Preston, 127
McClure, Edith, 83, 112
McDermet, Beth, 97
McDermet, Kris, 105, 175
McNamara, Sarah J., 46, 125
McNerney, Tom, 71, 77, 113, 163
Merikallio, Pat, 41, 117
Millen, JoAnn, 109
Millen, Lindsay, 90
Miller, Colleen J., 44
Miller, Joanne, 144
Miller, Tricia Tague, 31, 56, 64, 79, 83, 84, 98, 114
Mims, Lisa, 72, 89
Mohrmann, Joan, 44
Mollica, Andra, 171
Moore, Diane, 24, 59
Morgan, Elizabeth, 148, 165, 169, 173, 187
Munson, Carol M., 51, 53, 159
Norton, Nancy, 143, 159
Oberstar, Betty, 52
O'Brien, Diana, 101, 102
O'Brien, Liz, 110
O'Classen, Claire, 146
Ocone, Lynn, 146
O'Connor, Mary Lee, 56, 72, 184
Oken, Fran, 115
Oliver, Celia Y., 115
Olson, Bonnie, 101
Oxford, Amy, 99
Palmer, Joanna, 34, 45
Panaceck, Dorothy, 83, 108
Papetti, Gail, 141
Parker, Mary, 142
Patten, Kathleen, 22, 126, 171, 184
Payton, Tina, 74, 166
Peake, Milda, 107
Pelish, Lori Lupe, 122, 123
Petillo, Carol Morris, 50, 54, 58, 134, 154
Peyton, Janice, 183
Philbrick, Toni, 174
Phillips, Diane, 58, 156
Phillips, Nancy, 97
Pisanelli, Suzanne, 113
Podob, Laura, 73, 161
Pond, Barbara D., 37, 43
Poremski, Shelley, 60, 97
Prather, Suzi, 96, 98, 120, 164, 173
Pringle, Mary, 179
Province, Sarah, 141

Quigley, Karen, 65, 86, 90, 91, 111, 114, 115
Quintman, Judy, 50, 74, 113, 165
Rankin, Dorothy, 46
Reiber, Sandi, 106
Reinhart, Polly, 47, 110
Repasky, Linda, 69, 85, 91, 92, 93, 110
Reynolds, Gloria, 63, 188
Richards, Cynthia, 35
Ridgway, Lelia F., 138
Riley, Phyllis M., 38
Robertson, Emily, 26, 35, 179
Rogers, Julie, 86, 95
Rothschild, Olga, 179
Rotoli, Cynthia, 163
Rowe, Maureen, 178
Ruckert, Baily, 132, 140
Ryan, Carole J., 45
Ryder, Devin, 123
Santaniello, Janet, 112, 177
Sargent, Andrea, 49
Sargent, Mary, 41
Scanlon, Arlene, 139
Schmidt, Gail, 164
Scott, Louise, 102
Seward, Lucinda, 55, 76, 85, 96
Shaw, DonnaSue, 95, 104, 180
Shaw, Mildred H., 71
Sheldon, Linda Y., 108
Simpson, Victoria E., 145
Sly, Marilyn L., 39, 99
Smidt, Susan L., 72
Smith, Gwenn C., 105, 157, 174
Smith, Jean VanSchoonhoven, 48
Smith, Jule Marie, 1, 10-21, 188
Smith, Roberta, 94
Sousa, Dayne, 102, 158
Spokes, Amy, 136
St. George, Ruth, 37
Stanilonis, Peggy, 49
Stefanik, Donna Andrews, 165
Stoep, Paige Osborn, 156
Strack, Theresa, 39, 94
Strauss, Alberta, 142
Sybertz, Laurie M., 157
Taylor, Nancy L., 75
Thomann, Deb, 46, 50, 113, 117, 162
Toolin, Cynthia, 47
Toth, Cecelia K., 84, 103
Town, Sandra, 167
Townsend, Sharon L., 152, 160
Urbanak, Nancy, 57, 77, 169
Van Marter-Rexford, Melissa, 168, 182
Villavicencio, Rosario, 100
Varley, Patti, 55, 92
Wagemaker, Marty Dale, 25
Wagner, Dee, 78
Walden, Trish, 169
Walker, Claire, 136
Walsh, Deborah, 53, 163
Wheeler, Joan, 39, 132
White, Johanna, 84
Wiedemann, Shirley, 137
Wiles, Laurilyn, 121
Williams, Brenda C., 167
Williams, Janet, 82
Wilson, Robin, 36, 62
Winterling, Ann, 35
Wolfel, Helen, 130, 188
Wolfel, Luise, 32, 33
Yates, Maureen, 61, 127
Yoder, Patty, 23, 29
Zandy, Shirley H., 61, 182, 188
Zickler, Nancy, 2